OFFICIAL
SPECIMEN
QUESTION PAPER
AND HODDER GIBSON
MODEL QUESTION PAPERS
WITH ANSWERS

NATIONAL 5

HEALTH AND FOOD TECHNOLOGY

2013 Specimen Question Paper & 2013 Model Papers

HODDER
GIBSON
LEARN MORE

This book contains the official 2013 SQA Specimen Question Paper for National 5 Health and Food Technology, with associated SQA approved answers modified from the official marking instructions that accompany the paper.

In addition the book contains model practice papers, together with answers, plus study skills advice. These papers, some of which may include a limited number of previously published SQA questions, have been specially commissioned by Hodder Gibson, and have been written by experienced senior teachers and examiners in line with the new National 5 syllabus and assessment outlines, Spring 2013. This is not SQA material but has been devised to provide further practice for National 5 examinations in 2014 and beyond.

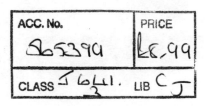
Hodder Gibson is grateful to the copyright holders, as credited on the final page of the Answer Section, for permission to use their material. Every effort has been made to trace the copyright holders and to obtain their permission for the use of copyright material. Hodder Gibson will be happy to receive information allowing us to rectify any error or omission in future editions.

Hachette UK's policy is to use papers that are natural, renewable and recyclable products and made from wood grown in sustainable forests. The logging and manufacturing processes are expected to conform to the environmental regulations of the country of origin.

Orders: please contact Bookpoint Ltd, 130 Park Drive, Abingdon, Oxon OX14 4SE. Telephone: (44) 01235 827720. Fax: (44) 01235 400454. Lines are open 9.00–5.00, Monday to Saturday, with a 24-hour message answering service. Visit our website at www.hoddereducation.co.uk. Hodder Gibson can be contacted direct on: Tel: 0141 848 1609; Fax: 0141 889 6315; email: hoddergibson@hodder.co.uk

This collection first published in 2013 by
Hodder Gibson, an imprint of Hodder Education,
An Hachette UK Company
2a Christie Street
Paisley PA1 1NB

BrightRED Hodder Gibson is grateful to Bright Red Publishing Ltd for collaborative work in preparation of this book and all SQA Past Paper and National 5 Model Paper titles 2013.

Typeset by PDQ Digital Media Solutions Ltd, Bungay, Suffolk NR35 1BY

Printed in the UK

A catalogue record for this title is available from the British Library

ISBN: 978-1-4718-0219-5

3 2 1

2014 2013

Introduction

Study Skills – what you need to know to pass exams!

Pause for thought

Many students might skip quickly through a page like this. After all, we all know how to revise. Do you really though?

Think about this:

"IF YOU ALWAYS DO WHAT YOU ALWAYS DO, YOU WILL ALWAYS GET WHAT YOU HAVE ALWAYS GOT."

Do you like the grades you get? Do you want to do better? If you get full marks in your assessment, then that's great! Change nothing! This section is just to help you get that little bit better than you already are.

There are two main parts to the advice on offer here. The first part highlights fairly obvious things but which are also very important. The second part makes suggestions about revision that you might not have thought about but which WILL help you.

Part 1

DOH! It's so obvious but …

Start revising in good time

Don't leave it until the last minute – this will make you panic.

Make a revision timetable that sets out work time AND play time.

Sleep and eat!

Obvious really, and very helpful. Avoid arguments or stressful things too – even games that wind you up. You need to be fit, awake and focused!

Know your place!

Make sure you know exactly **WHEN and WHERE** your exams are.

Know your enemy!

Make sure you know what to expect in the exam.

How is the paper structured?

How much time is there for each question?

What types of question are involved?

Which topics seem to come up time and time again?

Which topics are your strongest and which are your weakest?

Are all topics compulsory or are there choices?

Learn by DOING!

There is no substitute for past papers and practice papers – they are simply essential! Tackling this collection of papers and answers is exactly the right thing to be doing as your exams approach.

Part 2

People learn in different ways. Some like low light, some bright. Some like early morning, some like evening / night. Some prefer warm, some prefer cold. But everyone uses their BRAIN and the brain works when it is active. Passive learning – sitting gazing at notes – is the most INEFFICIENT way to learn anything. Below you will find tips and ideas for making your revision more effective and maybe even more enjoyable. What follows gets your brain active, and active learning works!

Activity 1 – Stop and review

Step 1

When you have done no more than 5 minutes of revision reading STOP!

Step 2

Write a heading in your own words which sums up the topic you have been revising.

Step 3

Write a summary of what you have revised in no more than two sentences. Don't fool yourself by saying, 'I know it but I cannot put it into words'. That just means you don't know it well enough. If you cannot write your summary, revise that section again, knowing that you must write a summary at the end of it. Many of you will have notebooks full of blue/black ink writing. Many of the pages will not be especially attractive or memorable so try to liven them up a bit with colour as you are reviewing and rewriting. **This is a great memory aid, and memory is the most important thing.**

Activity 2 — Use technology!

Why should everything be written down? Have you thought about 'mental' maps, diagrams, cartoons and colour to help you learn? And rather than write down notes, why not record your revision material?

What about having a text message revision session with friends? Keep in touch with them to find out how and what they are revising and share ideas and questions.

Why not make a video diary where you tell the camera what you are doing, what you think you have learned and what you still have to do? No one has to see or hear it but the process of having to organise your thoughts in a formal way to explain something is a very important learning practice.

Be sure to make use of electronic files. You could begin to summarise your class notes. Your typing might be slow but it will get faster and the typed notes will be easier to read than the scribbles in your class notes. Try to add different fonts and colours to make your work stand out. You can easily Google relevant pictures, cartoons and diagrams which you can copy and paste to make your work more attractive and **MEMORABLE**.

Activity 3 – This is it. Do this and you will know lots!

Step 1

In this task you must be very honest with yourself! Find the SQA syllabus for your subject (www.sqa.org.uk). Look at how it is broken down into main topics called MANDATORY knowledge. That means stuff you MUST know.

Step 2

BEFORE you do ANY revision on this topic, write a list of everything that you already know about the subject. It might be quite a long list but you only need to write it once. It shows you all the information that is already in your long-term memory so you know what parts you do not need to revise!

Step 3

Pick a chapter or section from your book or revision notes. Choose a fairly large section or a whole chapter to get the most out of this activity.

With a buddy, use Skype, Facetime, Twitter or any other communication you have, to play the game "If this is the answer, what is the question?". For example, if you are revising Geography and the answer you provide is "meander", your buddy would have to make up a question like "What is the word that describes a feature of a river where it flows slowly and bends often from side to side?".

Make up 10 "answers" based on the content of the chapter or section you are using. Give this to your buddy to solve while you solve theirs.

Step 4

Construct a wordsearch of at least 10 X 10 squares. You can make it as big as you like but keep it realistic. Work together with a group of friends. Many apps allow you to make wordsearch puzzles online. The words and phrases can go in any direction and phrases can be split. Your puzzle must only contain facts linked to the topic you are revising. Your task is to find 10 bits of information to hide in your puzzle but you must not repeat information that you used in Step 3. DO NOT show where the words are. Fill up empty squares with random letters. Remember to keep a note of where your answers are hidden but do not show your friends. When you have a complete puzzle, exchange it with a friend to solve each other's puzzle.

Step 5

Now make up 10 questions (not "answers" this time) based on the same chapter used in the previous two tasks. Again, you must find NEW information that you have not yet used. Now it's getting hard to find that new information! Again, give your questions to a friend to answer.

Step 6

As you have been doing the puzzles, your brain has been actively searching for new information. Now write a NEW LIST that contains only the new information you have discovered when doing the puzzles. Your new list is the one to look at repeatedly for short bursts over the next few days. Try to remember more and more of it without looking at it. After a few days, you should be able to add words from your second list to your first list as you increase the information in your long-term memory.

FINALLY! Be inspired...

Make a list of different revision ideas and beside each one write **THINGS I HAVE** tried, **THINGS I WILL** try and **THINGS I MIGHT** try. Don't be scared of trying something new.

And remember – "FAIL TO PREPARE AND PREPARE TO FAIL!"

National 5 Health and Food Technology

Candidate guidance

This information is provided to offer you guidance when answering questions in the Specimen Question Paper and Model Papers in this book. It also explains what SQA markers will be looking for when they mark your work in the final exam.

The answers provided in this book are written to assist in determining the 'minimal acceptable answer', rather than to list every possible correct and incorrect answer.

Types of questions

There are five main types of question used in these question papers. Each assesses a particular skill, namely ability to:

- State/give/name/identify…
- Describe…
- Explain…
- Make adaptations…
- Evaluate the suitability of…

State/give/name/identify…

Questions that ask you to *state/give/name/identify…* require you to list a number of relevant items or facts up to the total mark allocation. These should relate to the context of the question and do not need to be in any particular order.

Describe

Questions that ask you to *describe…* require you to give an account of points which should relate to the question. They need not be in any particular order. You may provide several straightforward points or a smaller number of developed points, or a combination of these up to the total mark allocation for this question.

> *Example*
>
> Question: Describe one way the cake could be stored to keep it in good condition.
>
> Answer: Store in an airtight container/wrap in foil/ cling film.
>
> *One mark is awarded for the correct description of method of storage.*

Explain…

Questions that ask you to *explain…* require you to make the relationship between things clear, for example by giving accurate relevant points and showing connections between these and the context of the question. You can provide several straightforward explanations or a smaller number of developed explanations, or a combination of these up to the total mark allocation for this question.

> *Example*
>
> Question: Explain two ways in which the man could use the information on food labels to help him make healthier food choices.
>
> Answer: He could check to see how much fat/sugar/ salt/fruit/vegetables is in the product so he can choose/avoid these.
>
> *One mark is awarded for each accurate, relevant point linked to the context of the question.*

Make adaptations…

Questions that ask you to *make adaptations…* require you to make a number of adjustments to improve the dish/recipe given in the question. You may provide a number of adaptations to meet given requirements and will normally be expected to explain the purpose of each up to the mark allocation for this question.

> *Example*
>
> Question: What adaptations could be made (to a given recipe) to help meet current dietary advice?
>
> Answer: The bacon could be grilled instead of fried. This would meet current dietary advice to eat less fat.
>
> *One mark is awarded for a relevant adaptation. A second mark is awarded for any adaptation that is explained in relation to the requirements of the question, as in the example above.*

Evaluate the suitability of...

Questions that ask you to *evaluate the suitability of…* require you to provide a number of evaluative comments which make a judgment based on the information provided and related to the context of the question. You may provide several straightforward observations or a smaller number of developed observations, or a combination of these up to the mark allocation for this question:

Example

Question: Taking account of the Dietary Reference Values (DRVs) for males aged 50 plus, comment on the suitability of his day's meals.

Answer: His intake of sodium is too high and this will make his high blood pressure worse. This will increase his risk of a stroke.

One mark is awarded for a relevant evaluative comment linked to the context of the question. A second mark is awarded for any evaluative comment that is developed, as in the example above.

Good luck!

Remember that the rewards for passing National 5 Health and Food Technology are well worth it! Your pass will help you get the future you want for yourself. In the exam, be confident in your own ability. If you're not sure how to answer a question, trust your instincts and just give it a go anyway. Keep calm and don't panic! GOOD LUCK!

2013 Specimen Question Paper

N5

National Qualifications
SPECIMEN ONLY

Mark

SQ22/N5/01

Health and Food Technology

Date — Not applicable

Duration — 1 hour and 30 minutes

Fill in these boxes and read what is printed below.

Full name of centre

Town

Forename(s)

Surname

Number of seat

Date of birth

Day	Month	Year
D D	M M	Y Y

Scottish candidate number

Total marks — 50

Attempt ALL questions.

Use **blue** or **black** ink.

Before leaving the examination room you must give this booklet to the Invigilator.
If you do not, you may lose all the marks for this paper.

MARKS | DO NOT WRITE IN THIS MARGIN

Question 1

> A school canteen supervisor wants to increase the amount of fruit and vegetables the pupils eat.

(a) Name **two** nutrients which can be found in fruit and vegetables and explain at least **one** function of **each** in the diet.   4

Nutrient 1 _____

Explanation(s) _____

_____

_____

_____

_____

Nutrient 2 _____

Explanation(s) _____

_____

_____

_____

_____

MARKS

Question 1 (continued)

> Many school children do not like eating whole fruit and vegetables.

(b) State **two** practical ways the canteen supervisor could include fruit or vegetables in the menu to encourage pupils to eat them.   **2**

Practical way 1 _____

_____

_____

Practical way 2 _____

_____

_____

(c) Describe **one** step the canteen supervisor should take when preparing or cooking vegetables and explain why this would make sure they keep as much of their nutritional content as possible.   **2**

Step _____

_____

_____

Explanation _____

_____

_____

MARKS | DO NOT WRITE IN THIS MARGIN

Question 1 (continued)

(d) Describe **two** duties of the Environmental Health Department in relation to food premises.   **2**

1 _____

_____

_____

2 _____

_____

_____

Total marks 10

MARKS | DO NOT WRITE IN THIS MARGIN

Question 2

> A food manufacturer wants to extend their range of baked products to include fruit cakes.

(a) State **two** reasons for carrying out market research for the new product.   2

Reason 1 _____

_____

_____

Reason 2 _____

_____

_____

The results of prototype production show the following problems with the cakes.

> **Results of prototype production**
> i.   Cakes are too crisp around the edges when baked.
> ii. The fruit has sunk to the bottom of the cakes.
> iii. Cakes have not risen enough.

(b) Explain why **each** of these problems may have happened.   3

(i) _____

_____

_____

(ii) _____

_____

_____

(iii) _____

_____

_____

MARKS | DO NOT WRITE IN THIS MARGIN

Question 2 (continued)

A consumer wants to buy a birthday cake for a child who will be three on 25th July and is having a birthday party on that date where there will be 10 guests.

(c) Identify the most suitable cake for the consumer to buy from the three shown below.

Features	Cake A	Cake B	Cake C
Sizes available	10–12 portions	18-20 portions	8-10 portions
Type of cake	Sponge	Sponge	Fruit and nut
Fillings	Buttercream and jam	Buttercream	No filling
Decoration	Large range of children's themes available	Range of cartoon characters available	Can be personalised by the consumer
Shelf life	Best before 27 July	Best before 25 July	Best before 26 July
Cost	££	£££	££

Key:

£ ――――→ ££££
Inexpensive   Expensive

(i) State **the most suitable** cake for the consumer to buy for the birthday party.   1

_____

MARKS DO NOT WRITE IN THIS MARGIN

Question 2 (c) (continued)

(ii) Considering all of the features described in the table above, give **three** reasons for your choice of cake.   3

_____

_____

_____

_____

_____

_____

_____

_____

(d) Describe **one** way the cake could be stored to keep it in good condition.   1

_____

_____

_____

Total Marks 10

MARKS

DO NOT WRITE IN THIS MARGIN

Question 3

> A young business woman has little time to shop for food and eats too many takeaway meals. She would like to shop for food online and make healthier dishes at home.

(a) Evaluate the suitability of this method of shopping for her using the features listed below.

4

Online shopping

- **Food items are arranged in virtual 'aisles'**
- **Your last order is displayed automatically**
- **Special offers displayed on the website home page**
- **Delivery is available 8am - 6pm, seven days a week**
- **You can choose a two hour delivery slot**
- **Substitute items will be sent automatically**
- **Free delivery if your order is over £100**

Evaluation _____

_____

_____

_____

_____

_____

_____

_____

_____

_____

MARKS | DO NOT WRITE IN THIS MARGIN

Question 3 (a) (continued)

_____

_____

_____

_____

_____

_____

_____

She would like to make a healthier version of her favourite takeaway baguette at home.

Bacon Baguette

Fried streaky bacon
Onion
Cheddar cheese
Mayonnaise
Salt
White baguette

(b) Describe **three** changes she could make and explain how **each** change helps to meet a different piece of current dietary advice.

6

Change 1 _____

_____

_____

Explanation _____

_____

_____

MARKS

Question 3 (b) (continued)

Change 2 _____

_____

_____

Explanation _____

_____

_____

Change 3 _____

_____

_____

Explanation _____

_____

_____

Total marks 10

MARKS | DO NOT WRITE IN THIS MARGIN

Question 4

A company which specialises in organic produce currently sells organic meat and vegetables. They plan to expand their business to include:

- organic meat boxes which are delivered direct to the consumer;

- a range of ready meals which use their produce.

As part of their market research the company have developed an organic meat box which they plan to trial with consumers.

(a) Make **four** evaluative comments about the suitability of the organic meat box.

4

Organic Meat Box

Contents:

- minced beef

- a whole chicken

- a variable selection of ready meals which use our organic meat and vegetables

- all produce is certified organic standard

- all meat is produced within 20 miles

- recipes are available on our website

- delivered weekly

- a seasonal organic vegetable box can be bought for half price if ordered with meat

MARKS | DO NOT WRITE IN THIS MARGIN

Question 4 (continued)

Evaluation

Point 1 _____

_____

_____

_____

Point 2 _____

_____

_____

_____

Point 3 _____

_____

_____

_____

Point 4 _____

_____

_____

_____

MARKS | DO NOT WRITE IN THIS MARGIN

Question 4 (continued)

The company wants to develop a range of ready meals which include their organic meat and vegetables.

(b) Identify **two** steps they might carry out in the product development process and explain how these could help the company make a successful food product. **4**

Step _____

Explanation(s) _____

_____

_____

Step _____

Explanation(s) _____

_____

_____

MARKS | DO NOT WRITE IN THIS MARGIN

Question 4 (continued)

The company has put the following labels on two of the ready meals.

(c) Explain what the information on **each** of these labels tells the consumer.

   (i) Food product – Frozen organic beef burgers

Best before:
January 2015

   (ii) Food product – Chilled organic vegetable lasagne

Use by:
12 June

(i) _____

_____

_____

(ii) _____

_____

_____   2

Total marks 10

MARKS | DO NOT WRITE IN THIS MARGIN

Question 5

> A 51 year old office worker works long hours. He is overweight and has high blood pressure and wants to improve his diet.

Dietary Reference Values for Males aged 50+ years					
Estimated average requirements	Reference Nutrient intakes				Guideline daily amount
Energy (MJ)	Protein (g)	Vitamin B complex (mg)	Iron (mg)	Sodium (g)	Fibre (g)
10·60	53·3	1·4	8·7	1·6	18

The table below shows the dietary analysis of a typical day's meals for the man.

Dietary analysis of his typical day's meals					
Energy (MJ)	Protein (g)	Vitamin B complex (mg)	Iron (mg)	Sodium (g)	Fibre (g)
13·20	55·0	1·6	4·8	2·1	12

(a) Taking account of the Dietary Reference Values (DRVs) for males aged 50 plus, evaluate the suitability of his typical day's meals.

6

Evaluation _____

_____

_____

_____

_____

_____

_____

_____

_____

_____

MARKS

Question 5 (continued)

_____

_____

_____

_____

_____

_____

_____

_____

_____

_____

_____

_____

_____

(b) Explain **two** ways in which the man's long working hours could influence his choice of foods.

2

1 _____

_____

_____

2 _____

_____

_____

MARKS | DO NOT WRITE IN THIS MARGIN

Question 5 (continued)

(c) Explain **two** ways in which the man could use the information on food labels to help him make healthier food choices.

2

1 _____

_____

_____

_____

2 _____

_____

_____

_____

Total marks 10

[END OF SPECIMEN QUESTION PAPER]

NATIONAL 5

2013 Model Paper 1

HODDER
GIBSON
LEARN MORE

NATIONAL 5
HEALTH AND FOOD TECHNOLOGY 2013   28   HODDER GIBSON MODEL PAPERS

National Qualifications
MODEL PAPER 1

Health and Food Technology

Duration — 1 hour and 30 minutes

Total marks — 50

Attempt ALL questions.

Use **blue** or **black** ink.

MARKS | DO NOT WRITE IN THIS MARGIN

Question 1

> A sports centre cafe wants to increase the range of sandwiches that it offers in its menu.

(a) Name **one** nutrient which can be found in bread and explain its function in the diet.

2

Nutrient _____

Explanation(s) _____

_____

_____

_____

> Tom is a 17-year-old school pupil who eats in the sports centre cafe. His hobbies include playing 5-a-side football and swimming.

Dietary Reference Values for males aged 15 – 18					
Estimated Average Requirements	Reference Nutrient Intakes				Guideline Daily Amount
Energy (MJ)	Protein (g)	Calcium (mg)	Vitamin B1 (mg)	Iron (mg)	Fibre (g)
11.54MJ	55.2g	1000mg	1.1mg	11.3g	18g

Dietary Analysis of his typical day's meals					
Estimated Average Requirements	Reference Nutrient Intakes				Guideline Daily Amount
Energy (MJ)	Protein (g)	Calcium (mg)	Vitamin B1 (mg)	Iron (mg)	Fibre (g)
10.78 MJ	74g	1035 mg	1.4 mg	8.9mg	15g

MARKS

Question 1 (continued)

(b) Taking account of the Dietary Reference Values (DRVs) for this age group, **evaluate** the suitability of this day's nutritional intake for Tom.   **6**

Evaluation _____

_____

_____

_____

_____

_____

_____

_____

_____

_____

_____

_____

_____

_____

_____

_____

_____

_____

_____

_____

_____

MARKS

DO NOT
WRITE IN
THIS
MARGIN

Question 1 (continued)

(c) Explain **two** ways that the sports centre cafe could address the
contemporary issue of sustainability.   **2**

Explanation 1 _____

_____

_____

_____

Explanation 2 _____

_____

_____

_____

Total marks 10

MARKS | DO NOT WRITE IN THIS MARGIN

Question 2

(a) A student wants to buy a readymade meal. Study the information about readymade meals below and choose the **most suitable** for the student.

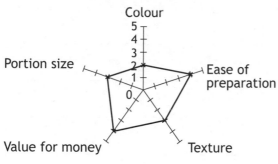

Ready made meal A

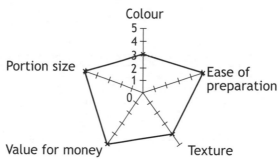

Ready made meal B

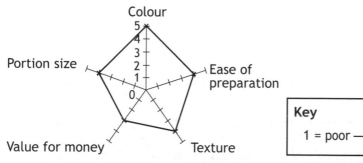

Ready made meal C

Key

1 = poor ⟶ 5 = excellent

(i) State the most suitable ready-made meal for the student to buy.   **1**

_____

MARKS

Question 2 (a) (continued)

(ii) Considering all of the factors, give **three** reasons for your choice of ready-made meal for the student.   3

_____

_____

_____

_____

_____

_____

_____

_____

_____

(b) Explain the importance of **each** of the following stages in product development.   2

Concept generation

Explanation_____

_____

_____

_____

First production run

Explanation_____

_____

_____

_____

MARKS

Question 2 (continued)

(c) Identify **two** points of information which, by **law**, must be stated on a food label.   **4**

Explain the importance of **each** point to the consumer.

Point 1 _____

Explanation _____

_____

_____

_____

_____

Point 2 _____

Explanation _____

_____

_____

_____

_____

Total marks 10

MARKS | DO NOT WRITE IN THIS MARGIN

Question 3

(a) A student is going to a music festival with a friend. She intends to camp there for two nights. Evaluate the suitability of the breakfast product below for a student.   **3**

No added sugar
Pack contains 6 individually wrapped bars
Eat straight from the packet
No refrigeration required
Varieties available: apple, cranberry, cherry
Contains artificial colours and flavours

Evaluation _____

_____

_____

_____

_____

_____

_____

_____

_____

_____

_____

(b) Explain the interrelationship between calcium and vitamin D.   **1**

_____

_____

_____

_____

MARKS | DO NOT WRITE IN THIS MARGIN

Question 3 (continued)

(c) The students purchased a snack from a catering van at the music festival.

An Environmental Health Officer inspected the catering van and found the following situations.

---

1. **Raw meat and vegetables being prepared using the same knife.**

2. **Hot food being placed in the refrigerator to cool down.**

For **each** of these situations identify **one** potential food hygiene hazard and give **one** solution to each.   4

Potential food hygiene hazard 1 _____

Solution 1 _____

_____

_____

Potential food hygiene hazard 2 _____

Solution 2 _____

_____

_____

(d) Give **one** advantage and **one** disadvantage to the consumer of buying genetically modified food.   2

Advantage _____

_____

_____

_____

Disadvantage _____

_____

_____

_____

Total marks 10

MARKS | DO NOT WRITE IN THIS MARGIN

Question 4

(a) The school canteen supervisor wishes to adapt the following macaroni cheese recipe to help meet current dietary advice.

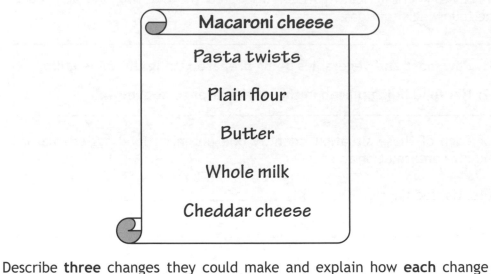

Macaroni cheese

Pasta twists

Plain flour

Butter

Whole milk

Cheddar cheese

Describe **three** changes they could make and explain how **each** change helps to meet a different piece of current dietary advice.   6

Change 1 _____

_____

_____

Explanation _____

_____

_____

Change 2 _____

_____

_____

Explanation _____

_____

_____

MARKS | DO NOT WRITE IN THIS MARGIN

Question 4 (a) (continued)

Change 3 _____

_____

_____

Explanation _____

_____

_____

(b) Explain how changing the proportion of ingredients in the following products served in the school canteen would affect the finished result.   **2**

Increase the proportion of flour in a sauce.

Explanation _____

_____

_____

Increase the proportion of fat in pastry.

Explanation _____

_____

_____

(c) Explain two ways in which the technological development of vacuum packing can help prevent food spoilage in the canteen.   **2**

Explanation 1 _____

_____

_____

Explanation 2 _____

_____

_____

Total marks   10

MARKS | DO NOT WRITE IN THIS MARGIN

Question 5

(a) A manufacturer wishes to extend his range of healthy eating products to include "ready to steam" meals. The target market is consumers who:

- are health conscious
- enjoy food that is aesthetically pleasing
- have little time for food preparation
- want value for money.

Information about "ready to steam" meals			
	Meal A	**Meal B**	**Meal C**
Main ingredients	• chicken • mushrooms • brown rice	• ham • cheddar cheese • pasta	• beef • chilli sauce • egg noodles
Aesthetic appeal	★★★★	★★★★	★★★★
Storage	Keep refrigerated for up to 5 days. Suitable for freezing. May be cooked from frozen.	Keep refrigerated for up to 6 days. Not suitable for freezing.	Keep refrigerated for up to 3 days. Packaged in a protective atmosphere for freshness.
Preparation	Remove outer packaging. Pierce film. Place in steamer for 15 minutes (25 minutes if frozen). Stir contents. Serve.	Remove outer packaging. Transfer to a heatproof container. Place in steamer for 25 minutes. Finish under grill to brown. Serve.	Remove outer packaging. Remove packet of chilli sauce. Pierce film. Place in steamer for 15 minutes. Stir in chilli sauce. Steam for a further 5 minutes. Serve.
Cost	££	££	£££

Key:

£ ——————→ ££££
Inexpensive   Expensive

(i) State the most suitable "ready to steam" meal for the manufacturer to develop.

1

_____

MARKS

Question 5 (a) (continued)

(ii) Considering all the features described in the table on page 12, give three reasons for your choice of "ready to steam" meal.

3

_____

_____

_____

_____

_____

_____

_____

_____

_____

_____

(b) Explain **two different** factors that influence consumer food choice.

2

Factor 1 _____

Explanation _____

_____

_____

_____

Factor 2 _____

Explanation _____

_____

_____

_____

MARKS

DO NOT
WRITE IN
THIS
MARGIN

Question 5 (continued)

(c) Steaming is a cooking method that can help prevent obesity.

Explain **two** other methods of cooking that can contribute to the reduction of obesity.   4

Method 1 _____

Explanation _____

_____

_____

_____

_____

Method 2 _____

Explanation _____

_____

_____

_____

_____

Total marks 10

[END OF MODEL PAPER]

2013 Model Paper 2

National Qualifications
MODEL PAPER 2

Health and Food Technology

Duration — 1 hour and 30 minutes

Total marks — 50

Attempt ALL questions.

Use **blue** or **black** ink.

MARKS | DO NOT WRITE IN THIS MARGIN

Question 1

(a) A school canteen supervisor wishes to extend the range of healthy eating sandwiches.

Study the information about sandwiches shown below and choose the **most suitable** to be sold in the school canteen.

Sandwich Information		
Sandwich A	Sandwich B	Sandwich C
Cheddar cheese with pickle on a white roll	Crispy bacon, tomato, hardboiled egg with butter on granary bread	Tuna, onions, sweetcorn with low fat mayonnaise on wholegrain bread

(i) State the most suitable sandwich for the school canteen.   1

_____

(ii) Considering all of the information above, give **three** reasons for your choice of sandwich for the school canteen.   3

_____

_____

_____

_____

_____

_____

_____

_____

_____

_____

MARKS

DO NOT
WRITE IN
THIS
MARGIN

Question 1 (continued)

(b) Explain why the following stages in food product development would be important for the canteen to consider before adding a new food product to the menu.   **3**

Concept Screening

Explanation _____

_____

_____

_____

Prototype Production

Explanation _____

_____

_____

_____

Product Testing

Explanation _____

_____

_____

_____

(c) State **two** ways the school canteen could reduce food waste during production.   **2**

Way 1 _____

_____

_____

Way 2 _____

_____

_____

MARKS | DO NOT WRITE IN THIS MARGIN

Question 1 (continued)

(d) The label displayed below is found on sandwich packaging. Explain what this tells the consumer.

1

Explanation _____

_____

_____

_____

_____

Total marks 10

Question 2

Mr and Mrs Patel are a retired couple. They need a fridge freezer for their large kitchen. They do a large fortnightly shop. They often have leftovers which they freeze.

Study the information about the fridge freezer below.

Fridge Freezer Information

- Extra large storage shelves
- Vitamin fresh storage*
- Temperature display on door
- Stainless steel doors
- Auto defrost
- Water and ice dispenser
- Hygiene active system**
- Large freezer section

Key:
 * fruit and vegetables are kept fresher for up to 3 times longer
** refreshes the air in the fridge section every 20 minutes, removing any bacteria

MARKS | DO NOT WRITE IN THIS MARGIN

Question 2 (continued)

(a) **Evaluate** the suitability of the fridge freezer for Mr and Mrs Patel.   **3**

Evaluation _____

_____

_____

_____

_____

_____

_____

_____

_____

_____

_____

_____

(b) The fridge freezer develops a fault and Mr and Mrs Patel discover that the fridge freezer was 'reconditioned'* and not 'new' as described by the trader. Explain **two** actions that the Trading Standards Department may take.   **2**

> * reconditioned refers to a product that has previously been sold to a consumer, returned due to a fault and then fixed and re-sold by the manufacturer. This product must be declared reconditioned and not sold as new.

Action 1_____

_____

_____

_____

Action 2_____

_____

_____

_____

MARKS

Question 2 (continued)

(c) A manufacturer wants to introduce a range of "Food-to-go" lunch boxes for the elderly.

The food must:

- be international
- be ready to eat
- be aesthetically pleasing
- provide value for money
- have recyclable packaging.

Study the information about the "Food-to-go" lunch boxes below and choose the most suitable to be sold.

Information about "Food-to-go" lunch boxes			
	Lunch box A	**Lunch box B**	**Lunch box C**
Packaging	• cardboard box with plastic inner sections • wooden chopsticks • soy sauce sachet	• waxed cardboard box with cardboard dividers • wooden fork • paper napkin	• polystyrene tray with cellophane wrap • plastic cutlery • moist wipe in foil sachet
Contents	• Chinese rice salad • prawn crackers • lychees	• Italian pasta salad • mini bread sticks • watermelon slices	• Scotch egg salad • ready salted crisps • apple
Appearance	★★★★	★★★★	★★★
Flavour	★★	★★★	★★★
Cost	£££	££	££

Key:

★ ⟶ ★★★★   £ ⟶ ££££

Poor ⟶ Excellent   Inexpensive ⟶ Expensive

(i) State the most suitable lunch box meal to be sold.

_____

MARKS | DO NOT WRITE IN THIS MARGIN

Question 2 (c) (continued)

    (ii) Considering all of the factors, give **three** reasons for your choice of lunch box meal.

        3

_____

_____

_____

_____

_____

_____

_____

_____

_____

  (d) Name the organisation which protects the consumer when buying food.   1

_____

Total marks 10

MARKS

Question 3

Max, a 34-year-old long-distance lorry driver, is slightly overweight and has a history of high blood pressure in his family. He eats most of his meals at a roadside café and spends his leisure time playing pool.

Dietary Reference Values for men aged 19 – 50 years					
Estimated Average Requirements	Reference Nutrient Intakes				Guideline Daily Amount
Energy (MJ)	Protein (g)	Sodium (mg)	Vitamin A (Ug)	Iron (mg)	Fibre (g)
11.5MJ	55.5g	1600 mg	700 Ug	8.7mg	18

Dietary Analysis of his typical day's meals					
Energy (MJ)	Protein (g)	Sodium (mg)	Vitamin A (Ug)	Iron (mg)	Fibre (g)
9.5MJ	59.9g	1641 mg	539 Ug	5.43mg	15g

MARKS | DO NOT WRITE IN THIS MARGIN

Question 3 (continued)

(a) Taking account of the Dietary Reference Values (DRVs) for this age group, **evaluate** the suitability of this day's nutritional intake for Max.   6

Evaluation _____

_____

_____

_____

_____

_____

_____

_____

_____

_____

_____

_____

_____

_____

_____

_____

_____

_____

_____

_____

_____

MARKS | DO NOT WRITE IN THIS MARGIN

Question 3 (continued)

(b) Explain how the following factors could influence a consumer's choice of food.   **2**

Advertising / media _____

_____

_____

_____

Allergies _____

_____

_____

_____

(c) Identify one sensory test a manufacturer could carry out when developing a new product for consumers and explain what information they would get from it.   **2**

Sensory Test _____

Explanation _____

_____

_____

_____

Total marks 10

MARKS | DO NOT WRITE IN THIS MARGIN

Question 4

(a) Name **two** nutrients that can be found in red meat and explain at least one function of each in the diet.   **4**

Nutrient 1_____

Explanation(s)_____

_____

_____

_____

_____

Nutrient 2_____

Explanation(s)_____

_____

_____

_____

_____

(b) **Other than diet**, explain **two different** factors which may contribute to obesity.   **2**

Explanation 1_____

_____

_____

_____

Explanation 2_____

_____

_____

_____

MARKS | DO NOT
WRITE IN
THIS
MARGIN

Question 4 (continued)

(c) Explain **four** points of advice to follow when barbequing food to reduce the risk of food poisoning.   4

Point 1 _____

Explanation _____

_____

_____

_____

Point 2 _____

Explanation _____

_____

_____

_____

Point 3 _____

Explanation _____

_____

_____

_____

Point 4 _____

Explanation _____

_____

_____

_____

MARKS | DO NOT WRITE IN THIS MARGIN

Question 5

(a) A local manufacturer wants to change the ingredients in the fish pie recipe below to help meet current dietary advice.

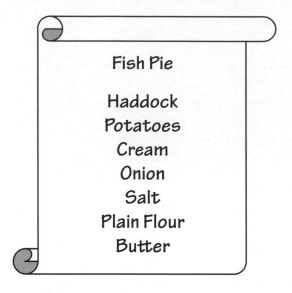

Fish Pie

Haddock
Potatoes
Cream
Onion
Salt
Plain Flour
Butter

Describe **three** changes the manufacturer could make and explain how **each** change helps to meet a different piece of current dietary advice.   **6**

Change 1 _____

_____

_____

Explanation _____

_____

_____

Change 2 _____

_____

_____

Explanation _____

_____

_____

MARKS | DO NOT WRITE IN THIS MARGIN

Question 5 (a) (continued)

Change 3_____

_____

_____

Explanation_____

_____

_____

(b) The manufacturer plans to sell the product at local farmers' markets. Explain at least **one** advantage and **one** disadvantage for consumers of shopping at farmers' markets.   **2**

Advantage(s)_____

_____

_____

_____

Disadvantage(s)_____

_____

_____

_____

(c) State **two** benefits to the consumer of using cook-chill products.   **2**

Benefit 1_____

_____

_____

_____

MARKS | DO NOT WRITE IN THIS MARGIN

Question 5 (c) (continued)

Benefit 2_____

_____

_____

_____

Total marks   10

[END OF MODEL PAPER]

2013 Model Paper 3

HODDER
GIBSON
LEARN MORE

N5

National
Qualifications
MODEL PAPER 3

Health and Food
Technology

Duration — 1 hour and 30 minutes

Total marks — 50

Attempt ALL questions.

Use **blue** or **black** ink.

MARKS

Question 1

(a) Explain **two** reasons why a manufacturer may want to develop a new product.

2

Reason 1_____

_____

_____

Reason 2_____

_____

_____

(b) A mobile catering company has been asked to provide take-away food at a family fun day. They wish to buy a range of burgers to sell at the event.

Study the information about the burgers below and choose the most suitable range for the company to buy.

Information about Burgers				
	Burger A	**Burger B**	**Burger C**	**Burger D**
Varieties available	• beef	• beef • chicken • spicy bean	• beef • chicken • quorn	• beef • venison • bacon
Burger weights available	50 g	50 g 100 g	50 g 100 g	100 g 150 g
Value for money	★★	★★★	★★★	★★
Storage details	• refrigerate • use within 3 days	• frozen • defrost before use	• frozen • can be cooked from frozen	• refrigerate • can be frozen
Aesthetic appeal	★★	★★★	★★★★	★★★
Key: ★ ⟶ ★★★★ Poor ⟶ Excellent				

MARKS | DO NOT WRITE IN THIS MARGIN

Question 1 (b) (continued)

    (i) State the most suitable burger for the company to buy.   **1**

    _____

    (ii) Considering all the features described in the table on page two, give **three** reasons for your choice of burger.   **3**

    Reason 1 _____

    _____

    _____

    Reason 2 _____

    _____

    _____

    Reason 3 _____

    _____

    _____

(c) The mobile catering van is also going to introduce a new range of milk and yoghurt drinks to its menu.

Name **two** nutrients which can be found in dairy products and **explain** at least **one** function of each in the diet.   **4**

Nutrient 1_____

Explanation(s)_____

_____

_____

_____

Nutrient 2_____

Explanation(s)_____

_____

_____

_____

Total marks 10

MARKS | DO NOT WRITE IN THIS MARGIN

Question 2

Susan is a 32-year-old vegan. She is five months pregnant. She has had to give up work and spends a lot of time reading.

Dietary Reference Values for females 19 — 50 years					
Estimated Average Requirements	Reference Nutrient Intakes				Guideline Daily Amount
Energy (MJ)	Protein (g)	Calcium (mg)	Vitamin C (mg)	Iron (mg)	Fibre (g)
1.94 MJ	45 g	700 mg	40 mg	14.8 mg	18 g

Dietary Analysis of her typical day's meals					
Energy (MJ)	Protein (g)	Calcium (mg)	Vitamin C (mg)	Iron (mg)	Fibre (g)
2.02 MJ	28 g	560 mg	44 mg	9.8 mg	21 g

(a) Taking account of the Dietary Reference Values (DRVs) for this age group, **evaluate** the suitability of her typical day's meals.

6

Evaluation_____

_____

_____

_____

_____

_____

_____

_____

_____

_____

MARKS DO NOT WRITE IN THIS MARGIN

Question 2 (a) (continued)

_____

_____

_____

_____

_____

_____

A food manufacturer wants to extend its range of cook-chill products to include a range for pregnant women.

(b) Explain **two different** sensory evaluations that the manufacturer could carry out to ensure that it makes a successful food product.　2

Sensory evaluation 1_____

_____

_____

_____

Sensory evaluation 2_____

_____

_____

_____

MARKS | DO NOT WRITE IN THIS MARGIN

Question 2 (continued)

(c) Following the sensory evaluation, the manufacturer has decided to include a baked quiche in its cook-chill range for pregnant women. The ingredient list is shown below.

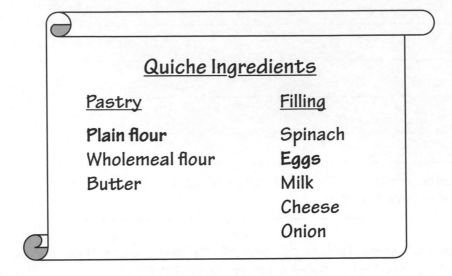

Quiche Ingredients

Pastry	Filling
Plain flour	Spinach
Wholemeal flour	**Eggs**
Butter	Milk
	Cheese
	Onion

Explain the functional properties of the ingredients below when cooking the quiche   2

Plain flour _____

_____

_____

_____

Eggs _____

_____

_____

_____

Total marks 10

MARKS | DO NOT WRITE IN THIS MARGIN

Question 3

(a) A chef is developing a new fruit ice lolly for children. The results of sensory testing are shown below.

Information about Fruit Ice Lollies

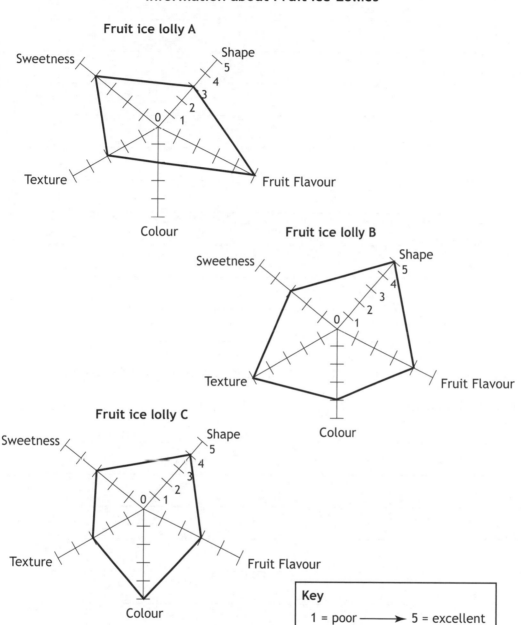

Key

1 = poor ⟶ 5 = excellent

(i) State the most suitable ice lolly for the chef to make.   1

_____

MARKS | DO NOT WRITE IN THIS MARGIN

Question 3 (a) (continued)

(ii) Considering all of the factors on page seven, give **three** reasons for your choice of ice lolly.

3

Reason 1 _____

_____

_____

_____

Reason 2 _____

_____

_____

_____

Reason 3 _____

_____

_____

_____

(b) Explain how the following factors may influence parental food choice.

2

Nutritional knowledge _____

_____

_____

_____

Budget _____

_____

_____

_____

(c) Explain **two advantages** and **one disadvantage** to the consumer of food additives.

3

Advantage 1 _____

_____

_____

_____

MARKS

DO NOT WRITE IN THIS MARGIN

Question 3 (c) (continued)

Advantage 2 _____

_____

_____

_____

_____

Disadvantage 1 _____

_____

_____

_____

_____

(d) Name the organisation responsible for ensuring that food additives used in the manufacture of food products are not harmful.   **1**

_____

Total marks 10

MARKS | DO NOT WRITE IN THIS MARGIN

Question 4

Current Dietary Advice states we have to increase the intake of oily fish in the diet.

(a) Explain **three** benefits to health of increasing oily fish in the diet.   3

Benefit 1 _____

_____

_____

_____

Benefit 2 _____

_____

_____

_____

Benefit 3 _____

_____

_____

_____

(b) Explain how the three types of information on food labels listed below help the consumer make an informed choice when comparing similar food products.   3

List of ingredients _____

_____

_____

_____

Weight / volume _____

_____

_____

_____

MARKS | DO NOT WRITE IN THIS MARGIN

Question 4 (b) (continued)

Country of origin _____

_____

_____

_____

(c) A television company has asked a celebrity chef to develop a dish which he will demonstrate on a cookery programme.

The dish must be:

- suitable for vegetarians
- quick and easy to prepare and cook
- aesthetically pleasing
- inexpensive.

Information about dishes			
	Dish A	**Dish B**	**Dish C**
Main ingredients	• spaghetti • tomatoes • mushrooms • mince	• macaroni • cream • peas • cheese	• tagliatelle • tomatoes • peppers • cheese
Ease of preparation	★★★	★★★★	★★★★
Cooking Time	20 minutes	30 minutes	20 minutes
Flavour	★★	★★	★★★
Aesthetic appeal	★★★★	★★★	★★★★
Cost	££££	£££	£££

Key:

★ ⟶ ★★★★   £ ⟶ ££££

Poor ⟶ Excellent   Inexpensive ⟶ Expensive

(i) State the most suitable dish for the chef to cook.   1

_____

MARKS | DO NOT WRITE IN THIS MARGIN

Question 4 (c) (continued)

(ii) Considering all of the factors on page eleven, give **three** reasons for your choice of dish for the chef to cook.   3

Reason 1 _____

_____

_____

_____

_____

Reason 2 _____

_____

_____

_____

_____

Reason 3 _____

_____

_____

_____

_____

Total marks 10

MARKS

Question 5

(a) State **three** pieces of current dietary advice (**other than increasing oily fish**).

Give a **different** practical way of meeting **each** piece of advice.   6

Current dietary advice 1 _____

_____

_____

Practical way_____

_____

_____

Current dietary advice 2_____

_____

_____

Practical way_____

_____

_____

Current dietary advice 3_____

_____

_____

Practical way_____

_____

_____

MARKS | DO NOT WRITE IN THIS MARGIN

Question 5 (continued)

(b) State **one** advantage and **one** disadvantage of buying foods online.   **2**

Advantage _____

_____

_____

_____

Disadvantage _____

_____

_____

_____

(c) Explain **two** ways that dental caries can be prevented.   **2**

Explanation 1 _____

_____

_____

_____

Explanation 2 _____

_____

_____

_____

Total marks 10

[END OF MODEL PAPER]

NATIONAL 5 | ANSWER SECTION

SQA AND HODDER GIBSON NATIONAL 5 HEALTH AND FOOD TECHNOLOGY 2013

NATIONAL 5
HEALTH AND FOOD TECHNOLOGY
SPECIMEN QUESTION PAPER

There are five types of question used in this question paper. Each assesses a particular skill, namely:

    A: State/give/name/identify
    B: Describe
    C: Explain
    D: Make adaptations to…
    E: Evaluate the suitability of…

For each question type, the following provides an overview of the marking principles and an example of their application for each type.

Questions that ask candidates to state/give/name/identify
Candidates should list a number of relevant items or facts. These should relate to the context of the question and do not need to be in any particular order.

Questions that ask candidates to describe
Candidates must define or give an account of points which should relate to the question. They need not be in any particular order. Candidates may provide a number of straightforward points or a smaller number of developed points, or a combination of these.

- 1 mark should be awarded for each accurate relevant point of knowledge linked to the context of the question.

Question: Describe **one** way the cake could be stored to keep it in good condition.

Example: *Store in an airtight container/wrap in foil/cling film.* (1 mark for correct description of method of storage.)

Questions that ask candidates to explain
Candidates should make the relationship between things clear, for example by giving accurate relevant points showing connections between these and the context of the question. Candidates may provide a number of straightforward explanations or a smaller number of developed explanations, or a combination of these.

- 1 mark should be awarded for each accurate relevant point.

Question: Explain **two** ways in which the man could use the information on food labels to help him make healthier food choices.

Example: *He could check to see how much fat/sugar/salt/fruit/vegetables is in the product so he can choose/avoid these.* (1 mark for accurate relevant point linked to the context of the question.)

Questions that ask the candidate to make adaptations to…
Candidates should make a number of adjustments to improve the dish/recipe given in the question. Candidates may provide a number of adaptations to meet given requirements and would normally be expected to explain the purpose of each.

- 1 mark should be awarded for each relevant adaptation.
- A second mark should be awarded for any adaptation that is explained in relation to the requirements of the question as in the following example.

Question: What adaptations could be made (to a given recipe) to help meet current dietary advice?

Example: *The bacon could be grilled instead of fried* (1 mark for adaptation). *This would meet current dietary advice to eat less fat* (a second mark for detail linked to the relevant current dietary advice).

Questions that ask the candidate to evaluate the suitability of…
Candidates should make a number of evaluative comments which make a judgment based on the information provided, related to the context of the question. Candidates may provide a number of straightforward observations or a smaller number of developed observations, or a combination of these.

- 1 mark should be awarded for each relevant evaluative comment linked to the context of the question.
- A second mark should be awarded for any evaluative comment that is developed, as in the following example:

Question: Taking account of the Dietary Reference Values (DRVs) for males aged 50 plus, comment on the suitability of his day's meals.

Example: *His intake of sodium is too high and this will make his high blood pressure worse.* (1 mark for comment) *This will increase his risk of a stroke.* (A further mark for the development of the comment.)

1. (a) Candidates should list a number of relevant facts and provide further explanation related to the facts listed.

    Candidates may provide a number of facts, or a smaller number of developed points or a combination of these.

    Candidates can be credited in a variety of ways up to a maximum of 4 marks.

    Candidates should list up to two nutrients found in fruit and/or vegetables. Candidates should explain the function in the diet of the nutrient specified.

    1 mark should be given for each correct response made, up to a maximum of **4 marks** in total:

    - a maximum of **2 marks** may be awarded for correctly identified nutrients
    - a maximum of **2 marks** may be awarded for correct explanation linked to any one of the identified nutrients

    For example, candidate could provide *either*:

    - **two** nutrients, **each with one** correctly explained function
    or
    - **two** nutrients, with **two correctly explained functions for one** nutrient

Nutrients	Function in the diet
Vitamin A/ carotene/ retinol	• promotes good night vision • maintains healthy membranes • helps to resist infection • helps with bone and tooth development
Vitamin B complex	• release of energy from food • required for cell reproduction • required for function of the nervous system
Vitamin C	• helps to absorb iron from food • helps prevent infection • helps heal cuts and wounds
Iron	• required for making red blood cells • prevents anaemia
Carbohydrate	• source of energy • warmth • excess is stored as fat • can act as a protein sparer
Protein	• growth and repair • maintenance of body tissues • secondary source of energy

Note: Other acceptable nutrients and their functions can be awarded marks.

(b) Candidates should make a number of relevant points. These should relate to the question.

Candidates can be credited in a number of ways up to a maximum of 2 marks.

Candidates should describe a number of practical ways to include fruit and vegetables in the menu.

1 mark should be given for each correct response made, up to a maximum of **2 marks in total**:

• a maximum of **2 marks** may be awarded for correct practical ways of including fruit in the menu
• a maximum of **2 marks** may be awarded for correct practical ways of including vegetables in the menu

For example, candidate could provide *either*:

• 2 responses linked for fruit *or*
• 2 responses linked to vegetables *or*
• 1 response linked to fruit and 1 response linked to vegetables
(up to a maximum of 2 marks)

Vegetables
• make vegetable soup
• add to stew/casseroles/curry/pizza/pasta dishes
• add a side salad to main meals/salad pots
• add to baked products (eg carrot cake)

Fruit
• make smoothies
• add to baked products (eg apple cake, banana loaf)
• offer fresh fruit juice
• add to desserts (eg yoghurt)

(c) Candidates should give a detailed account of relevant points. These should relate to the question.

Candidates can be credited up to a maximum of 2 marks.

Candidates must describe a relevant method of retaining nutrients when preparing/cooking vegetables.

• Maximum of **1 mark** may be awarded for correct description of method of preparation/cooking to retain nutrients.
• Maximum of **1 mark** may be awarded for correct explanation relating to the described method of preparation/cooking.

Step when preparing/ cooking	Explanation
• buy as fresh as possible • do not store for long periods • peel thinly/do not peel • do not chop finely	Vitamin C is lost through oxidation/ to the air.
• cook in a minimum amount of water • steam or microwave • keep the lid on the pan	Vitamins B complex and C are water soluble.
• cook for the minimum amount of time • serve immediately • do not keep warm	Vitamin C is destroyed by heat.

(d) Candidates should make a number of factual relevant points. These should relate to the question.

Candidates can be credited up to a maximum of 2 marks.

Candidates should describe the duties of the EHD in relation to food premises.

1 mark should be given for each correct response made up to a maximum of **2 marks in total**:

• a maximum of **2 marks** may be awarded for correct interpretation of the duties of the EHD in relation to food premises

Duties of Environmental Health Department
• to enforce the Food Safety Act 1990 • to carry out a routine check of premises/ practices • to investigate complaints about standard of hygiene from the public • to inspect food in the premises • to take away suspect food for testing • to carry out a risk assessment • to give advice to the owner/manager • to check that food for sale is fit for consumption • to find the source of an outbreak of food poisoning • to help avoid an outbreak of food poisoning

2. (a) Candidates should make a number of points that make the issue plain or clear, for example by showing connections between reason and the context of the question.

Candidates can be credited up to a maximum of 2 marks.

Candidates must describe a number of relevant reasons for using market research.

1 mark should be given for each correct reason up to a maximum of **2 marks in total**:

- a maximum of **2 marks** may be awarded for correct reason for the use of market research

Market research
• to identify if there is a gap in the market for the product
• to identify market trends for this type of product
• to find if the product is likely to sell
• to find out the kind of people who might buy the product
• to help establish the price of the product
• in response to consumer/suggestions
• to match a competitor's product
• to increase market share
• to evaluate a current product's performance
• so the product is more likely to be successful
• to increase sales/profit
• to avoid making a product which does not sell

(b) Candidates should make a number of points that make the issue plain or clear, for example by showing connections between the reason and the context of the question.

Candidates can be credited up to a maximum of 3 marks.

Candidates should give a number of relevant explanations for the outcomes in the question.

1 mark should be given for each accurate explanation up to a maximum of **3 marks in total**.

Too crisp round the edges when baked
• oven temperature too high
• cake too close to the side of the oven
• cake too high in oven
• cake baked for too long
• too much sugar
Fruit has sunk to the bottom
• mixture too soft
• too much liquid added
• fruit wet when added
• fruit not coated with flour before adding to mixture
• oven temperature too low
Has not risen enough
• plain flour used
• not enough raising agent
• raising agent out of date/damp
• mixture not beaten enough
• oven temperature too low

(c) Candidates should list a number of relevant facts and provide further justification related to the facts listed.

Candidates may provide a number of explanations for the identified fact, or a smaller number of developed points, or a combination of these.

Candidates can be credited in a number of ways up to a maximum of 4 marks.

Candidates should identify the most suitable cake. Candidates could provide a number of accurate explanations to justify their choice.

1 mark should be given for each accurate response up to a maximum of **4 marks in total**:

- **1 mark** should be awarded for correct choice of cake – Cake A.
- **1 mark** should be awarded for each relevant reason offered in support of the candidate's choice of cake, up to the total mark allocation. Some examples of valid reasons are given below. Where all reasons relate to one feature (eg size), a maximum of 2 marks should be awarded for reasons offered.

For example, in respect of the correctly identified cake, candidates could provide *either*:

- **three** reasons each linked to a different aspect of the cake *or*
- **two** reasons linked to one aspect of the cake plus one reason linked to a different aspect of the cake

(up to a maximum of four marks)

Where a candidate identifies an incorrect cake:

- no marks should be awarded for choice
- one mark should be awarded for each relevant reason offered in support of the choice provided:
  o the aspect identified is the best or equal best reason
  o the link to the case study is relevant

(up to a maximum of 2 marks)

Most suitable cake is cake A
Cake size: 10-12 portions
• there will be enough cake to suit the number of people at the party • there will be little/no waste as there are 10 guests • there will be a little left over in case there is an extra guest
Type of cake: Sponge
• most children like sponge cake, so they are likely to enjoy this cake • there is no fruit/nuts which children may not like • there are no nuts to which children may be allergic • the cake will most likely be eaten preventing waste/saving the parent money
Filling: buttercream and jam
• most children will like the filling, so will enjoy the cake • most children will like filling, so there is less likely to be waste/save consumer money
Decoration: large range of children's themes available
• the cake will likely appeal to the child • the consumer will be more likely to be able to choose a theme that appeals to the child
Shelf life—best before 27th July
• the cake will keep fresh until the party • the consumer will not have to return to the store to buy the cake closer to the day of the party • any cake left over from the party will be able to be kept for a few more days • any leftover cake is less likely to be wasted • any leftover cake will still safe to eat
££—one of the least expensive cakes
• consumer may see this as good value for money • less likely to be too expensive for the consumer/more likely to be within the consumer's budget

(d) Candidates should list a relevant fact related to the question.

Candidates can be credited up to a maximum of 1 mark.

Candidates should provide an accurate description of one aspect of storage related to the cake.

• **1 mark** should be awarded for correct description.

Storing cake
• store in an airtight container/wrap in foil/cling film • store in a cool dry place • do not keep beyond the best before date

3. (a) Candidates should make a number of evaluative comments related to the context of the question.

Candidates may provide a number of straightforward evaluations or a smaller number of developed evaluations, or a combination of these.

*Candidates can be credited in a number of ways **up to a maximum of 4 marks**.*

Candidates should make evaluative comments on the suitability of the given aspects of online shopping related to the individual in the case study.

1 mark should be given for each accurate response up to a maximum of **4 marks in total**:

• a maximum of **four marks** may be awarded for valid evaluative comments relating to the given aspects of online shopping
• a maximum of **two marks** may be awarded for developed evaluations relating to the same identified aspects of online shopping

For example, the candidate could provide *either*:

• **four** evaluative comments **each** linked to a **different aspect** of online shopping *or*
• **two** evaluative comments linked to **each of two different aspects** of online shopping *or*
• **two** evaluative comments **each linked to a different aspect** of online shopping + **two** evaluative comments **linked to a third aspect** of online shopping

(up to a maximum of four marks)

Online food shopping
Food items are arranged in virtual 'aisles': • +ve—suitable as foods should be easier/quicker for her to find as foods of the same type will be together • +ve—suitable as will save her time because foods are grouped together • +ve—suitable as will be easier/quicker for her to find foods because foods are arranged like a supermarket Your last order is displayed automatically: • +ve—suitable as might save her time because she may buy the same things each time • +ve—suitable as it may make her less likely to forget items as this may remind her • -ve—not suitable as she might not save time if these are not products she wants this time Special offers displayed on the website homepage: • +ve—suitable as these might save her money if she wants the products offered • -ve—not suitable as she might not want the products • -ve—not suitable as she may be tempted to overspend/buy foods she does not need/cannot use before they go 'off' Delivery available 8am-6pm seven days a week: • +ve—suitable as she could arrange a time to suit her lifestyle as delivery is seven days a week • +ve—suitable as she could have her food delivered on her day off as delivery is seven days a week • -ve—not suitable as delivery 8am-6pm so she might not be in during the day

Online food shopping (continued)
You can choose a two-hour delivery slot:
- +ve—suitable as she could choose a two-hour delivery slot so she would not have to wait in too long for it to arrive
- -ve—not suitable as she has a busy lifestyle so she might not have time to wait in for two hours during the day

Substitute items will be sent automatically:
- +ve—suitable as substitute items are sent automatically so she will have a replacement for any items that are out of stock
- +ve—suitable as substitute item may save her time going to buy a replacement
- +ve—not suitable as the replacement items might not be appropriate

Free delivery if your order is over £100:
- +ve—suitable as free delivery on orders over £100 might save her money
- -ve—not suitable as her order might not be more than £100 so this will not be helpful
- -ve—not suitable as she may be tempted to buy more than she needs to trigger the free delivery

(b) Candidates should make a number of adjustments to improve the dish/recipe given in the question. Candidates should show connections between changes made and the context of the question.

Candidates can be credited up to a maximum of 6 marks.

The candidate should make relevant changes to the recipe in the question. The candidate could link the change to the appropriate current dietary advice.

1 mark should be given for each accurate response up to a maximum of **6 marks in total**:

- a maximum of **three marks** may be awarded for correct changes to the recipe
- a maximum of **three marks** may be awarded for correct link of identified change to current dietary advice

Adaptation	Current dietary advice met
• change streaky bacon for back bacon • trim excess fat off bacon • grill bacon instead of frying • replace cheddar cheese with edam/low fat cheddar • replace the mayonnaise with reduced fat mayonnaise	• eat less fat • reduce intake of fat • reduce intake of fat to no more than 35% of total energy • reduce intake of saturated fat • reduce intake of saturated fat to no more than 11% of total energy
• replace the white baguette with wholemeal/granary • increase the size of the baguette	• increase intake of fibre • eat more Total Complex Carbohydrates • eat more bread
• omit/reduce the salt	• eat less salt • reduce intake of salt

• increase amount of onion • add tomato/ mushrooms	• eat more fruit and vegetables • increase intake of fruit and vegetables to 400g/day/5 portions/day

4. (a) Candidates should make a number of evaluative statements related to the context of the question.

Candidates may provide a number of straightforward evaluations or a smaller number of developed evaluations, or a combination of these.

Candidates can be credited in a number of ways up to a maximum of 4 marks.

Candidates should make comments on the suitability of aspects of the organic meat box in relation to the case study.

1 mark should be given for each accurate response up to a maximum of **4 marks in total**:

- a maximum of **four marks** may be awarded for accurate evaluations relating to four aspects of the organic meat box
- a maximum of **two marks** may be awarded for developed evaluations relating to the same identified aspect of the organic meat box

For example, candidate could provide *either*:

- **four** evaluative comments **each** linked to a **different aspect** of the organic meat box *or*
- **two** evaluative comments linked to **each of two different aspects** of the organic meat box *or*
- **two** evaluative comments **each linked to a different aspect** of the organic meat box + **two** evaluative comments **linked to a third aspect** of the organic meat box

(up to a maximum of four marks)

Organic meat box
Contents:
- +ve - suitable as they get mince and chicken in each box so that will help them plan meals
- +ve - suitable as they get a variety of ready meals and they may like the idea of planning meals around them each time
- +ve - suitable as they may enjoy the variety of the items
- -ve - not suitable as they might not want to have the mince/chicken every time/may be wasted
- -ve - not suitable as they might not want to buy the variety of ready meals sent
- -ve - not suitable as they might not like the ready meals sent
- -ve - not suitable as they might not know how to prepare/cook some of the items
- -ve - not suitable as they might want to buy specific items which are not in the box/would need to order these separately

All produce is certified organic standard:
- +ve - suitable as they can be reassured of the organic origin of the meat
- -ve - not suitable as organic meat may be more expensive and they may not want the extra cost

All meat is produced within a radius of 20 miles:
- +ve - suitable as this will guarantee all items are produced locally/will support local producers
- +ve - suitable as they might be keen to save food miles/reduce carbon footprint
- +ve - suitable as they will know where the meat comes from

Recipes are available on company website:
- +ve - suitable as this may give them ideas for cooking the meat in the box
- +ve - suitable as this may help them prepare/cook any unfamiliar cuts/items
- -ve - not suitable as they may have to search for the recipes

Delivered weekly:
- +ve - suitable as it may contain enough meat for two people for one week
- -ve - not suitable as it may not contain enough meat for two people for one week
- -ve - not suitable as it may contain too much meat for two people for one week/meat may be wasted
- -ve - not suitable as it may contain too much meat for two people for one week/they may not have a freezer

Half-price seasonal organic vegetable box if ordered with meat:
- +ve - suitable as they may be keen to use organic vegetables
- +ve - suitable as this will save them money on vegetables
- +ve - suitable as this will save them time going elsewhere for vegetables
- -ve -not suitable if they do not wish to take advantage of the offer

(b) Candidates should list a number of relevant facts and provide further justification related to the facts listed.

*Candidates can be credited in a number of ways **up to a maximum of 4 marks**.*

Candidates should identify **two** steps in the product development process and explain their contribution to the potential success of the new product.

1 mark should be given for each correct response made, up to a maximum of **4 marks** in total:

- a maximum of **2 marks** may be awarded for correctly identified steps in the product development process
- a maximum of **2 marks** may be awarded for correct explanation linked to any one of the identified steps in the product development process

For example, candidate could provide *either*:

- **two** steps, **each with one** correct explanation *or*
- **two** steps, with **two correctly explained functions for one** step

(up to a maximum of four marks)

Steps	Developed points
Concept generation	• provide initial ideas for the new product • helps to establish if there is a gap in the market for the product
Concept screening	• best ideas are taken forward/less appropriate ideas are discarded so the product is more likely to be successful
Prototype production	• to test the production line to see if the product can be made successfully • to find out if the new product can be made at a cost at which it will sell/make a profit • to allow improvements to be made to the product so that it will sell better • to decide on the viability of the product
Product testing	• helps manufacturer to test for appeal • allows manufacturer to gain opinion of product • helps manufacturer to further refine product to improve
First production run	• manufacturer can see how popular the product is likely to be • the manufacturer can withdraw an unsuccessful product (if sales are not good) • the manufacturer can use sales figures to draw up a marketing plan to increase sales
Marketing plan	• decisions will be taken on how the product will be promoted to maximise sales • decisions will be taken on the price of the product so that is priced to sell well • decisions will be taken on the advertising of the product to increase sales • decisions will be taken on the packaging of the product to increase sales • decisions will be taken on the positioning of the product (for sale) so that it may sell more
Product launch	• product is promoted to the market to maximize sales • allows the manufacturer to judge consumer response and amend aspects of the product to increase sales

(c) Candidates must make a number of factual relevant points. These should relate to the question.

Candidates can be credited up to a maximum of 2 marks.

Candidates should provide an accurate explanation of implications of the labels.

1 mark should be given for each correct reason up to a maximum of **2 marks in total**:

- a maximum of **1 mark** may be awarded for correct explanation of implication of each label

> **Best before date**
> - products eaten after this date may have deteriorated but will still be safe to eat
> - product will have a medium/long shelf life
> - indicates the time within which the product is at its best in terms of taste/texture
>
> **Use by date**
> - products eaten after this time will cause food poisoning
> - indicates the product has a short shelf life/ requires refrigeration
> - indicates time within which the product is safe to eat/will not cause food poisoning

5. (a) Candidates should make a number of evaluative comments related to the context of the question.

Candidates may provide a number of straightforward evaluations or a smaller number of developed evaluations, or a combination of these.

Candidates can be credited in a number of ways up to a maximum of 6 marks.

Candidates should make comments on the suitability of aspects of the day's meals related to the individual in the case study.

- a maximum of **four marks** may be awarded for accurate evaluative comments relating to four different aspects of the day's meals related to the individual in the case study
- a maximum of **two marks** may be awarded for developed evaluations linked to the same identified aspect of the day's meals

For example, candidate could provide *either*:

- **four** evaluative comments each linked to a **different aspect** of the man's meals **(maximum of four marks)** *or*
- **two** evaluative comments linked to **each of three different aspects** of the man's meals **or**
- **two** evaluative comments **each linked to two different aspects** of the man's meals + **two** evaluative comments **linked to two further aspects** of the man's meals
(up to a maximum of six marks)

> **Energy —13·20MJ**
> - -ve — this has more energy than he needs so any extra will be converted to fat
> - -ve — this has more energy than he needs so making him more overweight
> - -ve — more energy than he needs will increase his weight and so increase his blood pressure
> - -ve — more energy than he needs will increase his weight and so increase his risk of CHD/stroke
> - -ve — he is unlikely to burn off the excess energy as he has a sedentary occupation

> **Protein—55·0g**
> - +ve — he will get enough protein for repair and maintenance of body tissues
> - -ve — extra protein will be converted to fat and contribute to his weight gain
>
> **Vitamin B complex—1·6mg**
> - +ve — there is enough for the release of energy from food to allow him to work
>
> **Iron—6·8mg**
> - -ve — this is less than he needs so he may feel tired
> - -ve — this is less than he needs so he may feel tired and be unlikely to exercise
> - -ve — this is less than he needs so he may suffer from anaemia
>
> **Sodium—2·1g**
> - -ve — this is high so will further increase his blood pressure
> - -ve — this is high so will further increase his risk of CHD/stroke
>
> **Fibre—12g**
> - -ve — this is low so he may feel hungry and snack on foods which will increase his weight
> - -ve — this is low so he may increase his risk of CHD/constipation/bowel disease

(b) Candidates should make a number of points that make the issue plain or clear, for example by showing connections between factors and the context of the question. These could show justification for the factor.

Candidates can be credited up to a maximum of 2 marks.

Candidates must explain a number of factors relating to his long working hours on his food choices.

1 mark should be given for each correct explanation made up to a maximum of **2 marks in total**:

- a maximum of **1 mark** may be awarded for each accurate explanation relating to influence on his food choice

> **Long working hours**
> - he works long hours so he may choose convenience foods
> - he may choose convenience foods which are often high in fat so he may put on more weight
> - he may choose convenience foods which are often high in salt which will contribute to his high blood pressure
> - he works long hours so may snack frequently on high fat/high sugar foods
> - frequent snacking may contribute to his weight gain
> - he may choose convenience foods which may be low in fruit and vegetables

(c) Candidates must make a number of factual relevant points. These should relate to the question.

Candidates may provide a number of facts, or a smaller number of developed points or a combination of these.

*Candidates can be credited **up to a maximum of 2 marks**.*

Candidates must make a number of factual points of information found on food labels.

1 mark should be given for each correct response made up to a maximum of **2 marks in total**:

- a maximum of **2 marks** may be awarded for accurate explanation of points of information linked to better food choices

---

Ingredients list
- he could check to see how much fat/sugar/salt/fruit/vegetables is in the product so he can choose/avoid these
- he could take account of the amount of an ingredient in a product

Net quantity/weight/volume of product
- he could check the amount of the product to help portion control
- he could check so that he buys just enough for his needs so he may be less likely to overeat

Date mark
- so he can calculate the shelf life of the food so he will not be tempted to eat food which he needs to be consumed before it goes out-of-date

Nutritional information
- he could check the energy/fat/sugar content and choose the lowest versions

Nutritional/health claims
- he could check these and choose products which would help improve his health

---

1. (a) *2 marks*

Nutrient — carbohydrate
Explanation
- source of energy
- warmth
- excess is stored as fat
- can act as a protein sparer

Nutrient — vitamin B1
Explanation
- release of energy from carbohydrates
- promotes growth and appetite
- maintains a healthy nervous system

Nutrient — vitamin B2
Explanation
- release of energy from carbohydrates, protein and fat
- maintains healthy skin and eyes

or any other nutrient found in bread with relevant explanation.

(b) *6 marks*

Energy — 10.78MJ
- -ive — **Less** energy than he needs so he may not have energy to take part in swimming and football.
- -ive — **Less** energy than he needs and as Tom plays football and swims which uses energy he may lose weight/become underweight.
- -ive — **Less** energy than he needs may result in lack of concentration/tiredness during the day at school.
- -ive — **Less** energy than he needs and energy is required for all physical activity/body activity/swimming /football

Fibre — 15g
- -ive — **Less** fibre than he needs so he may suffer from constipation/diverticular disease/bowel disorders
- -ive — **Less** fibre than he needs which means he might not have a feeling of fullness and snack on other foods which could cause him to become overweight/cause tooth decay (fibre slows down digestive system).

Protein — 74g
- +ive — **More** energy than he needs which can be used as a secondary source of energy when Tom is playing football / swimming
- +ive — **More** energy than he needs and as Tom will still be growing, he should have no growth/development problems/muscles will develop/grow properly.
- +ive — **More** energy than he needs and as Tom plays football and swims, should he receive any injuries the extra protein will ensure they will heal/repair normally.
- -ive — **More** energy than he needs so if Tom stops playing football/swimming then the excess protein would be converted to fat, leading to obesity (if not burned off).

Calcium — 1035mg
- +ive — **More** calcium than he needs which will ensure he has correct growth/development/formation/maintenance of strong bones and teeth as a teenager

- +ive — **More** calcium than he needs which will ensure the normal clotting of the blood if he gets injured when playing football/swimming.
- +ive — **More** calcium than he needs which will help to prevent osteoporosis in later life.

Vitamin B1 — 1.4mg
- +ive — **More** vitamin B1 that he needs which will help release carbohydrate from food and give him energy when playing football/swimming.
- +ive — **More** vitamin B1 that he needs which will ensure that he maintains good muscle tone when playing football/swimming (improve performance).
- +ive — **More** vitamin B1 that he needs which will release energy to prevent tiredness at school/football/swimming.

Iron — 8.9mg
- -ive — Less iron that he needs which may put Tom at risk of developing anaemia.
- -ive — Less iron that he needs which may make him tired when playing football swimming or at school.

(c) *2 marks*
Ways to address sustainability
- Use local suppliers to reduce air miles/support local business.
- Sell food with longest shelf life to avoid waste.
- Avoid using unnecessary packing when serving food products to reduce harm to the environment.
- Use packaging that is reusable/recyclable to reduce harm to the environment.
- Use fair trade ingredients to ensure that producers are protected from exploitation.
- Use up leftover ingredients in a new dish.
- Place food waste on compost heap/in compost bin.
- Store food in correct conditions to avoid waste.
- Only buy/cook food that is required for the cafe to reduce waste.
- Only peel foods with inedible skin.

2. (a) (i) *1 mark*
Correct choice of ready made meal for the student — **Ready Made Meal B**

(ii) *3 marks*
Texture
- 4/very good/second best score — the student is likely to enjoy the meal/there is likely to be little waste, so saving money.

Value for money
- 5/excellent/best score — The student is likely to be on a limited budget and the meal is within their price range.

Portion size
- 5/excellent/best score — there is likely to be enough for the student to eat and feel full/satisfied.
- 5/excellent/best score — there is less likely to be any left over, so the student is not wasting money.
- 5/excellent/best score — student is unlikely to have to buy any more food for that meal.

Colour
- 3/average score — likely to find the meal attractive/aesthetically appealing.
- 3/average score — the student may not find the meal as attractive as others and choose not to buy.

Ease of Preparation
- 5/excellent/best score — the meal will be quick to prepare and the student may be busy with coursework/studying.
- 5/excellent/best score — the student may have limited cooking skills and they will be able to make the meal with ease/their capabilities.
- 5/excellent/best score — the meal is likely to require little equipment to prepare and the student may have limited equipment available/money to purchase.

(b) *2 marks*
Concept generation
- Developing/brainstorming ideas for a new product.
- Helps to establish a gap in the market.
- Helps to develop ideas from market analysis.
- It is the first stage in the development process for a new product.
- Stage where all/new ideas are considered.

First production run
- Manufacturer can see how popular the product is likely to be.
- The manufacturer can withdraw/adapt an unsuccessful product (if sales are not good).
- Manufacturer can avoid spending more money on an unsuccessful product.
- The manufacturer can use sales figures to draw up a marketing plan.
- Manufacturer can test the production line.

(c) *4 marks*
Point – Ingredients list (in descending order)
Explanation
- The consumer can take account of likes/dislikes.
- The consumer can take account of allergies/intolerances.
- The consumer can take account of the proportion/amount of an ingredient in the product.
- The consumer can see if the product is suitable for a vegetarian.

Point – Name or description of food
Explanation
- So the consumer is not misled/is clear about what is being bought.
- Names of certain foods are prescribed by law so the consumer is not misled.
- So the consumer knows of any process the food has undergone (eg part-baked/dried/smoked).

Point – Net quantity/weight/volume of product
Explanation
- So the consumer can compare prices.
- So the consumer can calculate value for money.
- So the consumer can check if the package contains enough for their needs/how many to buy.

Point – Date mark
Explanation
Use by date
- So the consumer can calculate the shelf life of the food.
- So the consumer knows when the food will no longer be safe to eat/may cause food poisoning.
Best before date
- Tells the consumer the date until which the food has best appearance/flavour/texture/nutritional value.
- So the consumer knows when the food will not be/taste as good but will still be safe to eat.

Point – Storage instructions
Explanation
- So the consumer can store food to keep it in optimum condition.
- So the consumer can maximise the shelf life of the food.
- So the consumer can enjoy the food at its best.
- So the consumer can check if they have the correct storage facilities (accept appropriate examples eg freezer).

Point – Preparation/cooking instructions
Explanation
- So the consumer gets the best results/enjoys the product at its best.
- To ensure the product is safe to eat.
- So the consumer does not use the product wrongly (eg 'not suitable for microwaving').

Point – Name and address/contact details of the manufacturer/packer/seller
Explanation
- So the consumer can contact the manufacturer in case of complaint/enquiry.

Point – Place/country of origin
Explanation
- The consumer may wish to avoid products from a certain country.
- The consumer may wish to support a particular country (accept examples, eg Produce of Scotland).

3. (a) *3 marks*
    No added sugar
    - +ive – May encourage the student to eat the product as it is healthier/contributes to the dietary targets.
    - +ive – Suitable as the student may be less likely to suffer from dental caries/obesity in later life.
    - -ive – May discourage the student from eating the product as it may not be sweet enough.

    Pack contains 6 individually wrapped bars
    - +ive – Suitable pack size for both students that will last the duration of the music festival
    - +ive – Suitable as the product will be protected from germs if the student puts the bar in their pocket (to eat later).
    - +ive – Suitable as this would help keep the student's hands clean when at the festival
    - +ive – Suitable as this would be more hygienic as the student may not have washed their hands/less chance of bacteria being transferred to the food.
    - +ive – Individual portion will be suitable as it is for one person.
    - -ive – May not be suitable as the student may get bored with the flavour (and some may be wasted).

    Eaten straight from the packet
    - +ive – Suitable for students at the music festival who may not have dishes to serve / eat from
    - +ive – Saves time for the student at the music festival as this does not need preparation/washing up.

    No refrigeration required
    - +ive – Suitable as the students will not have access to a fridge to store the breakfast safely when camping.
    - +ive – Suitable as there will be less risk of food poisoning to the student.

- +ive – Suitable as the student may eat the product later in the day without the risk of food poisoning.
- +ive – Suitable as these may be stored with less risk of food poisoning (if not eaten straight away).

Variety of flavours available
- +ive – Suitable as the student will be able to find one he/she likes.
- +ive – Suitable as there is a range/three flavours available and the student may like a variety.
- +ive – Suitable as fruit flavours are likely to appeal to students.
- +ive – May not be suitable as the student may not find one he/she likes.
- -ive – May be less suitable as the student may get bored with the flavour (and some may be wasted).

Contains artificial colours and flavours
- -ive – May not be suitable as some students may be allergic to colours/flavours.
- +ive – May be suitable as the student may like the flavour/colour and will be encouraged to eat breakfast

(b) *1 mark*
- Vitamin D works with calcium to aid absorption/forms strong bones and teeth.
- Without Vitamin D the body cannot make use of the calcium in food.
- Without Vitamin D less calcium will be absorbed and this will affect the strength of bones and teeth.

(c) *4 marks*
Raw meat and vegetables being prepared using the same knife
Potential hazard
- Transfer of bacteria from raw meat to vegetables.
- Cross contamination of bacteria from raw meat to vegetables.
Potential solution
- Use separate knife for meat and vegetables.
- Wash knives (thoroughly) in hot soapy water between preparing meat and vegetables.
- Use colour coded knives.

Hot food being placed in the refrigerator to cool down
Potential hazard
- Temperature in fridge would increase, causing bacterial growth.
- Increase in fridge temperature could cause other (perishable) foods to go off.
- Fridge temperature may not be low enough to stop moulds/yeasts forming.
Potential solution
- Leave food to cool (at room temperature for a time) before putting in fridge.
- Keep fridge thermometer to ensure temperature is below 5°C.
- Have separate fridge/blast chiller for cooling hot food.

(d) *2 marks*
Advantages to the consumer
- Can assist in the preservation of food by preventing the ripening of fruits and vegetables enabling a longer shelf-life/increasing nutritional benefits. (helps to meet CDA).
- Can increase the variety of texture and appearances of food and so increase consumer choice.

- Can increase the shelf life of fresh foods without the use of preservatives or additives.
- Reduces crop waste and results in more stable prices of food.
- Some fruit and vegetables can be modified to contain higher level of nutrients, e.g. vitamins C and E. These vitamins could offer some extra protection against CHD and some cancers.
- Improvement in quality, flavour, crunchiness and texture of a wide range of foods, e.g. potatoes, tomatoes.

or any other relevant advantage.

Disadvantages to the consumer
- May be concerned about the ethical aspects of genetic modification and so not purchase food — the welfare of animals could be at risk.
- Religious beliefs may influence use of foods modified using genes from animals which are forbidden in some religions.
- Strict vegetarians would object to using copy genes of animal origin in a plant.
- Personal views / concern that food should be natural and not be tampered with.
- May be concerned about the environmental aspects of genetic modification and so not buy the food — genetically engineered plants and animals could affect wildlife.

or any other relevant disadvantage.

4. (a) *6 marks*

Change   **Add one (or more) vegetables to the dish (any suitable vegetable would be acceptable).**

Explanation — Fruit and vegetables
- Increase intake of fruit and vegetables.
- Increase intake of fruit and vegetables to 5 portions per day.
- Intake of fruit and vegetables to double.
- Intake of fruit and vegetables to increase to 400g per day.

Change   **Add (wholemeal) breadcrumbs as a topping to the dish/incorporate breadcrumbs into the sauce.**

Explanation — Bread
- Increase bread intake (mainly using wholemeal).
- Increase bread intake by 45%.

Change   **Add crushed breakfast cereals as a topping to the dish.**

Explanation — Breakfast cereals
- Increase intake of breakfast cereals.
- Intake of breakfast cereals to double.
- Intake of breakfast cereals to double to 34g per day.

Change   **Change butter to low fat alternative/ Change milk to semi-skimmed/Change cheese to reduced fat cheddar/edam/ gouda.**

Explanation — Fats
- Reduce intake of fat.
- Reduce total fat intake.
- Intake of total fat to be reduced to no more than 35% of food energy.
- Reduce intake of saturated fat.
- Average intake of saturated fat to be reduced to no more than 11% of food energy.

(b) *2 marks*

Increase the proportion of flour in a sauce
- The sauce will be thicker/more viscous.
- The sauce will gel.

Increase the proportion of fat in pastry
- Flavour will be richer.
- Pastry will be a darker colour.
- Pastry will be more fragile/crumbly.
- Pastry will be greasy.

(c) *2 marks*

Explanations
- Oxygen is removed so micro-organisms cannot multiply (unless anaerobic), preventing food spoilage.
- (Most) bacteria/micro-organisms cannot multiply without oxygen/air so food spoilage is reduced/ slowed down.
- Pack is sealed to prevent bacteria reaching the food so food spoilage is reduced slowed down.

5. (a) (i)   *1 mark*

Correct choice of "ready to steam" meal **A**

   (ii)   *3 marks*

Main ingredients
- Chicken/mushrooms/brown rice which will appeal to the target group who are health conscious.
- Chicken which is low in fat so will contribute to current dietary advice to reduce fat intake and appeal to the target group who are health conscious.
- Mushrooms which will contribute to the current dietary advice to increase intake of fruit and vegetables and appeal to the target group who are health conscious.
- Rice which will contribute to the dietary target to increase TCC and appeal to the target group who are health conscious.

Aesthetic appeal – 4 stars/excellent/best
- 4 stars/excellent/best rating so will appeal to the target group who enjoy food which is aesthetically pleasing.
- 4 stars/excellent/best rating so will encourage consumers to buy/make repeat purchases.
- 4 stars/excellent/best rating which is what is required by the manufacturer.

Storage – Keep refrigerated for up to 5 days/ suitable for freezing/may be cooked from frozen.
- Can be stored for up to five days so will appeal to the target group who have little time for food preparation as they may need to shop less frequently.
- Suitable for freezing so the target group can use it as required so saving time as they have little time for food preparation.
- Can be cooked from frozen so saving the target group time as they have little time for food preparation.
- Suitable for freezing so will save waste if the target group does not use it within 5 days, which will appeal as they want value for money.

Preparation – Remove outer packing. Pierce film. Place in steamer for 15 minutes (25 minutes if frozen). Stir contents. Serve.

- Quick/easy to prepare/cook which will appeal to the target group who have little time for food preparation.
- Little/no skill required so will appeal to the target group who have little time for food preparation.
- Shortest cooking time/one of the shortest cooking times even when frozen, so will appeal to the target group who have little time for food preparation.

Cost – ££/fairly inexpensive/one of the cheapest

- ££/fairly inexpensive/one of the cheapest so will be suitable for the target market who want value for money.
- ££/fairly inexpensive/one of the cheapest so the manufacturer may sell more (and increase profits).

(b) *2 marks*

Factor – Advertising, marketing and promotional techniques
Explanation

- The media, especially television, has a major influence on consumer food choice as it is used to promote different products aimed at their target markets.
- Advertising – brand loyalty may influence the consumer's food choice if they favour existing products.
- Promotional techniques are chosen with the target group in mind, e.g. free toys are often given with children's food products.

Factor – Available income
Explanation

- The amount of money available restricts the quantity, quality and variety of food which can be purchased.
- More high-fat and -sugar foods may be chosen if income is limited.as they are cheaper to purchase.
- Fruit and vegetables may not be purchased due to fear of waste.
- Untried foods may not be chosen for fear of waste if money is limited.
- Two or more salaries could also mean that more money may be available to buy more ready meals and convenience foods and these could be higher in fat and sugar.

Factor – Climatic conditions
Explanation

- Imported foods can mean that climate may have less influence on food choice.
- In cold weather there is a need for energy-giving and filling foods that will provide warmth to the body. In hot climates refreshing foods such as salad and fruit are popular.

Factor – Lifestyle
Explanation

- People want and enjoy more leisure time, so do not want to spend time preparing meals.
- People travel greater distances to work and so there is less time and energy for meal preparation.
- More women are now employed outwith the home and have less time for meal preparation.
- An increase in family income when both adults work means that they can afford the higher cost of ready-made meals.

- Consumers that have busy lifestyles want food that is easily consumed on the move, e.g. breakfast bars or ready-made sandwiches.
- More people live alone and want a choice of single-portion meals which are easy to prepare.
- 'Eating out' has increased and many restaurants have developed play areas for children which encourages families to eat out, often at a reasonable cost.
- People may not have the required food-preparation skills and so buy 'take-away' or ready prepared foods.

Factor – Nutritional knowledge
Explanation

- Food choice will be influenced by knowledge of the nutritional content of foods and its effects on health.
- There are now many low-fat options available because of the number of people who want to slim.
- Low-sugar foods are produced for people who are interested in reducing sugar intake.
- Low-salt foods are produced for people who want to reduce their intake of salt.

Factor – Environmental issues
Explanation

- Consumers are buying more natural, unprocessed food because of the fear of chemicals in food leading to carcinogens.
- Organic food is purchased because, during growth, only animal and vegetable waste materials are used instead of man-made chemicals/consumers think they taste better/are better for health.
- Consumers want to purchase foods that have recyclable packing as they may be conscious of the environment.

Factor – Foreign travel
Explanation

- More people travel abroad, where they have developed different tastes.
- There are now many ethnic groups in the UK who have greatly influenced our choice of foods and provide take-away/themed restaurants.

Factor – Geographical location/access to shops
Explanation

- Geographical location affects the purchasing of foods. Choice of foods will either be vast (as in the city) or very limited (as in small villages or towns).
- Geographical location may affect the range and frequency of delivery of fresh foods.
- Transport systems are now so well developed that it is possible for us in the UK to get fruits, vegetables and other foods flown in.
- Some people are confined to their local area when shopping for food because they have no private transport.
- The internet is fast becoming popular as a means of shopping by those people who have difficulty getting to the shops.
- Corner shops frequently keep hours which suit local lifestyles but costs are higher and the choice of products is smaller.

Factor – Health
Explanation

- The health of individuals at different stages of their lives will affect choice of foods, e.g. convalescents, pregnant women and the elderly may all have special nutritional requirements which will affect food choice.

- Allergies may restrict food choice, e.g. allergies to additives may also be common, particularly in children.
- Food intolerances to lactose will restrict the intake of milk and milk products. It is possible to buy lactose-reduced foods.

Factor – Peer pressure
Explanation
- The need for social acceptance and the imitation of one's peer group influences food choice.
- Influences from peer groups may affect a person's choice of diet.

Factor – Personal taste
Explanation
- If food looks attractive, smells appetising and tastes good then consumers are more likely to want it.
- Individual likes and dislikes within families can be passed from one generation to the next.

Factor – Preparation and cooking equipment available
Explanation
- Advances in technology have meant that food processors, mixers, blenders, and juicers have led to quicker and easier food preparation.
- Many new cooking appliances do the monitoring and timing of the cooking process, e.g. bread makers, ice-cream makers. This may encourage consumers to try these at home and produce a more 'home-made' product.

Factor – Preparation and cooking skills priorities
Explanation
- Loss of practical skills or limited practical skills in food preparation may mean that more ready-meals and take-away meals are used as an alternative to cooking.
- Reliance on convenience foods may mean that traditional food preparation and cooking skills are lost.
- Ready-prepared meals require no effort and are especially useful for people who are tired or in a hurry.
- People are now less willing to spend time on preparing food when working. They want to spend time on more leisure activities.

Factor – Shift patterns/working hours
Explanation
- Longer opening hours in all sections of industry and services mean that people have less time to prepare food.
- The increase in shift working has meant irregular eating patterns, with people in a household eating at different times of the day.

(c) *4 marks*
Method – grilling
Explanation
- Fat is removed from food during the cooking process as it drips from food into the grill tray when heated (prevents obesity).
- Dry method of cooking — no fat is added to food prior to cooking (prevents obesity).

Method – poaching
Explanation
- No fat is added during the cooking process. Food is cooked in a small amount of water (prevents obesity).

Method — stir frying
Explanation
- Only a small amount of oil/fat is required and food is cooked quickly over a high heat (prevents obesity).

Method — stewing / boiling / baking
Explanation
- No fat is added during the cooking process (prevents obesity).

NATIONAL 5 HEALTH AND FOOD TECHNOLOGY MODEL PAPER 2

1. (a) (i) *1 mark*
Correct choice **C**

(ii) *3 marks*
Tuna
- Good source of protein, required for growth of pupils.
- Oily fish helps pupils to meet Current Dietary Advice/eat two portions a week/double intake of oily fish.
- Good source of Vitamin A to help ensure pupils' resistance to infection/night vision/vision in dim light.
- Good source of Vitamin D to help ensure pupils form strong bones and teeth.

Onions and Sweetcorn
- Vegetables help pupils meet current dietary advice/5 portions per day/intake to double (to 400 grams per day).
- Sweetcorn good source of Vitamin C, needed by pupils to heal wounds/maintains the pupils' connective tissue/helps iron absorption/ prevents anaemia, common in teenagers/helps ensure pupils' resistance to infection.
- Good source of Vitamin B1 to release energy, which teenagers can use for exercise.
- Provide dietary fibre to help pupils avoid constipation/digestive disorders/cancers.

Low fat mayonnaise
- Reduced fat, helps to meet current dietary advice eat less fat/average intake of total fat to be reduced to no more than 35% of food energy.
- Reduced fat so helps pupils avoid obesity/ Coronary Heart Disease in later life.

Wholegrain bread
- Provides dietary fibre to help pupils avoid constipation/digestive disorders/cancers/bowel disease/bowel disorders.
- Helps pupils to meet current dietary advice to eat more bread/intake of bread to increase by 45%.
- Good source of Vitamin B to help pupils release energy from carbohydrate, which will assist all body functions.
- NSP/dietary fibre gives pupils a feeling of fullness so may help prevent them from snacking on high fat/high sugar foods.

(b) *3 marks*
Concept screening
- This stage is important, as it allows the production process to move away from initial ideas to actual development issues. (All ideas are considered — some kept and some discarded)
- Allows the manufacturer to develop a specification against which to develop ideas.
- Specification allows manufacturer to eliminate ideas that might be costly, difficult to process/not meet other constraints.
- Allow product ideas to be generated so that a prototype can be developed.

Prototype production
- The prototype is developed and measured against the specification (to ascertain if it meets the specification/further improvements to be made).
- The prototype is tested for appeal and may be further modified or rejected.

Product testing
- Allows the products to be tested on consumers, so opinions can be obtained.
- Allows the product to be further refined or eliminated as a result of consumer opinions.
- Allows the range of possible solutions to be further refined — the most suitable and popular product will be kept.

(c) *2 marks*
Ways to reduce food waste in the canteen
- Use a standardised recipe to ensure that quantities of ingredients aren't overused causing waste.
- Carry out efficient stock control of ingredients/ order only sufficient ingredients at a time.
- Carry out effective stock rotation (to avoid food spoilage)/Check efficient stock control of products and adjust production accordingly.
- Store food correctly to avoid waste/foods going off and having to be discarded.
- Carry out research to ensure that product meets pupil tastes.

(d) *1 mark*
Recycling label
- Shows that the item/packaging can be recycled/ used again.
- Shows that the item/packaging has been made from materials which have been recycled.
- Shows that the item/packaging is environmentally friendly.

2. (a) *3 marks*
Extra large storage shelves
- This is suitable for Mr and Mrs Patel as they do a large fortnightly shop so they can store large items/store large quantities of food/there will be enough space for all their food or drinks.
- This is suitable for Mr and Mrs Patel as they often have leftovers which they freeze so they can store large quantities of frozen food, which saves waste/ saves money.

Vitamin fresh storage
- This is suitable for Mr and Mrs Patel as they do a large fortnightly shop and the fruit and vegetables will stay in good condition, which will reduce food waste/save money.

Temperature display on door
- As Mr and Mrs Patel are retired they may spend a lot of time at home and will open/close the fridge door frequently — they can see that the fridge freezer is operating at the correct temperature.
- The temperature display will let Mr and Mrs Patel know that the food is being stored at the correct temperature and they can be confident that food is safe to eat. This will prevent food poisoning, which can be serious for the elderly.

Stainless steel doors
- The fridge freezer will last longer/be more durable/will not rust which will save money in replacing it.
- The fridge freezer will be easy to wipe/clean which is hygienic and less tiresome for the retired couple.

Auto defrost
- This is suitable as they are retired/they do a large fortnightly shop/as they often have leftovers which they freeze so will save them time/energy/be more convenient than defrosting manually (environmentally friendly).

Water and ice dispenser
- The fridge freezer has a water and ice dispenser this is suitable as it will save space in fridge/freezer when they do their large fortnightly shop

Hygiene active system
- When Mr and Mrs Patel do a large fortnightly shop the food will be stored safely. This reduces the risk of food going off and prevents waste

Large freezer section
- As they do a large fortnightly shop/often have leftovers which they freeze, they can store large quantities of frozen food/take advantage of special offers/buy in bulk and so save money.

(b) *2 marks*
Trading Standards Department Advice
Action points:
Any relevant answer relating to:
- Enforcing consumer protection laws and offer advice regarding purchases.
- Assisting traders in complying with relevant legislation (Sale and Supply of Goods Act).
- Investigate rogue traders to protect future/potential customers.
- Bring legal action to traders where necessary against trader for non-compliance to consumer protection laws/name of relevant law.

(c) (i) *1 mark*
Correct choice — Lunch Box **B**

(ii) *3 marks*
Packaging — waxed cardboard box with cardboard dividers/wooden fork/paper napkin
- Packaging can be recycled which is what the manufacturer wants/may appeal to consumers and so increase sales.
- Provides all materials needed to eat the meal.
- The wooden fork can be recycled which is what the manufacturer wants/may appeal to consumers and so increase sales.
- The paper napkin can be recycled which is what the manufacturer wants/may appeal to consumers and so increase sales.

Contents — Italian pasta salad, mini bread sticks, watermelon slices.
- No preparation required, which is what the manufacturer wants.
- Are all international which is what the manufacturer wants.
- All the foods are of Italian origin so are international.
- Meal is ready to eat which may appeal to consumers and increase sales.

Appearance — 4 rating stars/excellent/best
- More likely to choose the lunch box.
- More likely to enjoy the lunch box.
- May increase sales.

Flavour — 3 stars/good/second best rating
- More likely to enjoy the product.
- More likely to make repeat purchases and increase sales for the manufactures.

Cost — ££/inexpensive/one of the cheapest/best value
- May be more likely to buy it.
- May lead to increased sales and make a greater profit.

(d) *1 mark*
Organisation — Environmental Health Department

3. (a) *6 marks*
Energy — 9.5MJ
- -ive — Less energy than he needs and this could cause tiredness/lack of concentration when he is driving his lorry
- +ive — Less energy than he requires but as he leads a sedentary lifestyle Max may require less energy and this will help him lose weight/be less at risk from obesity

Fibre — 15g
- -ive — Less fibre than he needs and he may become constipated/suffer from bowel disease/diverticular disease (which will be uncomfortable when driving)
- -ive — Less fibre than he needs which slows down the digestive process and would make Max feel fuller for longer/he may be more likely to feel hungry and snack on foods/drinks high in fat/sugar, leading to obesity.

Protein — 59.9mg
- +ive — More protein than he requires but can be used as a secondary source of energy (energy level low for age group) to prevent tiredness.
- +ive — More protein than he requires, but if Max is in a driving accident the excess protein will help him heal.
- -ive — More protein than required which may be stored as energy. Due to sedentary lifestyle this may result in increased weight and lead to obesity.

Vitamin A — 539UG
- -ive — Less Vitamin A than he requires which may result in him developing cancer/heart disease in later life.
- -ive — Less Vitamin A than he needs and if driving at night his vision may not be good in the dark (possibly lead to a road accident).

Iron — 5.43mg
- -ive — Less iron than required which may result in anaemia/Max feeling tired when driving/playing pool

Sodium — 1641mg
- -ive — More sodium than required, which may cause him to develop high blood pressure/hypertension/stroke as it runs in his family (genetic).
- +ive — More sodium than required which will prevent Max from getting cramps when he is sitting for long periods of time while driving.

(b) *2 marks*

Advertising / media

- Increased advertising of healthy food products by the media could lead to an improvement in the diet of consumers.
- Adverts on television are shown at times when the target group will be watching television, so influences sales.
- Brand loyalty — consumers may purchase products because they are loyal to a particular brand.
- Media is now accessible on a wide variety of technological appliances and has a greater impact on consumers
- Reports and interviews on various topics, especially health, make consumers choose food differently. Articles may persuade consumers not to buy certain products because of negative publicity.
- A variety of promotional techniques are chosen with the target group in mind, e.g. free toys are often given with children's food products.
- Celebrities can be used to promote certain products to consumers.

Allergies

- Allergies to food may restrict food choice. Some consumers are allergic to peanuts and may suffer an anaphylactic reaction. These foods may be avoided by certain consumers.
- Allergies to additives are also common in consumers, particularly in children, and may encourage hyperactivity. As a precaution consumers may chose to buy foods that are additive-free.

(c) *2 marks*

Sensory Test – Preference/rating test
Explanation
- Collect information/opinions about specific attributes of a product.
- Identify specific strengths/weaknesses in a product.
- Allows changes to be made to specific attributes based on results of testing.

Sensory Test – Ranking/scoring/grading test
Explanation
- Find out how much a tester likes/dislikes a product.
- Make judgments about specific characteristics of a product, e.g. flavour/colour.

Sensory Test – Discrimination/difference test
Explanation
- Find out if testers can tell the difference between the manufacturer's product and that of a competitor.
- Find out if testers can tell the difference between an existing product and a new recipe.
- Find out if testers can tell the difference if the proportions of ingredients are changed, e.g. reduced salt.

Sensory Test – Paired comparison test
Explanation
- Find out if testers can tell the difference between two products in terms of a specific attribute, e.g. sweetness.
- Find out if testers can identify changes made in a recipe.

Sensory Test – Triangle test
Explanation
- Find out if testers can identify the product on test from two other similar products.
- Find out how similar/different the test product is from the other products.

Sensory Test – Taste threshold test
Explanation
- Find out the minimum concentration of an ingredient before the product becomes unacceptable.

4. (a) *4 marks*

Nutrient – Protein
Explanation
- growth, repair and maintenance of body tissues
- secondary source of energy

Nutrient – Fat
Explanation
- source of energy for the body
- warmth
- protection of internal organs
- provides fat soluble vitamins (A,D,E and K)

Nutrient – Iron
Explanation
- required for the formation of red blood cells
- Vitamin B
- release of energy from food
- maintain healthy nerves / cell production

Nutrient – Phosphorous
Explanation
- helps build strong bones and teeth
- helps to release energy from foods

Nutrient – Folic Acid
Explanation
- needed in the formation of fed blood cells
- reduces the risk of neural tube defects in pregnancy

Nutrient – Vitamin A (offal)
Explanation
- assists with bone and tooth development
- promotes good night vision
- maintains healthy skin/membranes/resist infection

Nutrient – Vitamin D (offal)
Explanation
- assists with bone and tooth development
- required for effective blood clotting
- assists in absorption of calcium

Nutrient – Vitamin B1 (offal)
Explanation
- release of energy from carbohydrates
- promotes growth
- maintains healthy nervous system

Nutrient – Vitamin B2
Explanation
- release of energy from protein, carbohydrate and fat
- maintains healthy skin and eyes

(b) *2 marks*

Activity/exercise
- Lack of exercise means that excess food/kJ is not burned off leading to obesity.
- More jobs are now sedentary so excess energy from food is converted to fat, which can lead to obesity.
- Increase in 'sedentary' pastimes (e.g. computer games/TV) using less energy so leading to obesity.
- People may drive/use public transport more so use up less energy, leading to obesity.

Lifestyle

- Increase in eating out/fast foods/takeaway may eat more food/more high-fat/sugar foods so contributing to obesity.
- Fewer 'family' meals/more 'grazing' so may choose high-fat/high sugar foods which contribute to obesity.
- More ready-made meals used which may be high in fat/sugar which contribute to obesity.

Hereditary/Genetics

- Obese parents may increase risk of obesity in their children.

Available income

- High available income may lead to the purchase of more food increasing the risk of obesity.
- High available income may lead to increase in eating out so increasing the risk of obesity.
- High available income may lead to purchase of more high fat/high sugar foods (e.g. cakes/ biscuits) so increasing the risk of obesity.
- Low available income may lead to reliance on high-fat/high sugar foods as 'fillers' so increase the risk of obesity.

Use of alcohol

- High consumption of alcohol will lead to high kJ intake increasing the risk of obesity.

Influence of advertising

- Can persuade consumer to make unwise choices high in fat/sugar (McDonalds/Irn-Bru adverts) which may contribute to obesity.
- May persuade consumer to visit fast food outlets which may only serve less healthy options so increasing the risk of obesity.

Influence of peers

- May persuade consumer to make poor food choices (high in fat) which contribute to obesity.

(c) *4 marks*

Point – Defrost meat/poultry/fish/burgers/sausages/ kebabs thoroughly.
Explanation
- If not defrosted then the food may not reach a high enough temperature to kill harmful bacteria in the centre (leading to food poisoning).
- Barbecued food may burn on the outside and still be raw in the centre not destroying harmful bacteria (leading to food poisoning).

Point – Keep food out of the danger zone/below 5°C and above 63°C before cooking/once cooked/ after cooking.
Explanation
- Bacteria multiply rapidly in the danger that may cause food poisoning.
- Keep perishable foods in the refrigerator below 5°C until ready for preparing/cooking/serving to keep food cool and prevent bacteria multiplying (leading to food poisoning).

Point – Cover all foods until ready for serving.
Explanation
- Keep raw meat in sealed containers away from ready to eat food to prevent cross contamination that could cause food poisoning.
- Cover foods before/during serving as flies, insects, birds, pets may spread harmful bacteria onto food leading to food poisoning/harmful bacteria may enter food and lead to food poisoning.

Point – Keep raw and cooked foods separately/ keep raw meat away from ready to eat food/don't put cooked food on surface used for raw meat/ store raw meat at bottom of fridge.
Explanation
- To prevent cross contamination from raw to cooked food which could cause food poisoning.

Point – Wash salads/fruits/vegetables before use.
Explanation
- To avoid the spread of harmful bacteria leading to food poisoning.
- To remove chemical or physical sources of contamination that could lead to food poisoning.

Point – Check use by dates on perishable foods.
Explanation
- To ensure bacterial count is within acceptable levels.

Point – Cook food thoroughly/to at least 75°C or above.
Explanation
- use temperature probe to check centre of food is at least 75°C to ensure that food in cooked through to centre to destroy harmful bacteria and prevent food poisoning.
- turn food regularly and move around the barbecue to cook evenly/until juices run clear to kill any harmful bacteria that may cause food poisoning.

Point – Reheat food only once.
Explanation
- Reheat food to 82°C (for at least 2 minutes) only once as harmful bacteria will have multiplied and may not be destroyed if food is heated more than once.

Point – Use separate utensils/chopping boards/ knives for raw and cooked food.
Explanation
- To avoid the spread of harmful bacteria from raw to cooked foods leading to food poisoning.
- To prevent cross contamination from raw to cooked food which can cause food poisoning.

Point – Ensure food handlers wash hands between touching raw and cooked food/visiting toilet/ touching bins.
Explanation
- To avoid the spread of harmful bacteria leading to food poisoning/to prevent cross contamination leading to food poisoning.

Point – Ensure food handlers follow rules on personal hygiene/wear a clean apron when preparing/cooking/serving food.
Explanation
- To prevent the food becoming contaminated with harmful bacteria which could lead to food poisoning.

Point – Food handlers preparing/cooking/serving food should not be suffering from infections/ diarrhoea/cuts.
Explanation
- This could lead to harmful bacteria being transferred from the food handler to the food leading to food poisoning.
- Cuts should be covered with a blue waterproof plaster to avoid physical contamination/harmful bacteria being passed from the food handler which could lead to food poisoning.

Point – Cool leftovers as quickly as possible, cover and refrigerate.

Explanation
- To prevent entry of harmful bacteria/prevent multiplication of harmful bacteria which may lead to food poisoning.

5. (a) *6 marks*

Change
- Add one (or more) vegetables to the dish (any suitable vegetable would be acceptable).
- Increase quantity of onion in the dish.

Explanation – Fruit and Vegetables
- Increase intake of fruit and vegetables.
- Increase intake of fruit and vegetables to 5 portions per day.
- Intake of fruit and vegetables to double.
- Intake of fruit and vegetables to increase to 400g per day.

Change
- Change cream to low fat alternative (Elmlea or similar).
- Replace cream with milk.
- Change butter to low fat alternative.
- Omit butter from sauce.

Explanation – Fats
- Reduce intake of fats.
- Reduce total fat intake.
- Intake of total fat to be reduced to no more than 35% of food energy.
- Reduce intake of saturated fat.
- Average intake of saturated fat to be reduced to no more than 11% of food energy.

Change
- Change white fish to oily fish (any oily fish would be acceptable).
- Increase quantity of fish in the dish.

Explanation – Fish
- Eat more fish, especially oily fish.
- Eat more oily fish.
- Intake of white fish to be maintained.
- Intake of oily fish to double (from 44g to 88g per week).

Change
- Remove salt from the dish.
- Replace with LoSalt/herbs.
- Reduce proportion of salt in the dish.

Explanation – Salt
- Intake of salt to be reduced.
- Intake of salt to be reduced from 163mmol per day to 100mmol per day/no more than 6g per day.

Change
- Increase potatoes in the dish.
- Add one (or more) vegetables to the dish (any suitable vegetable would be acceptable).
- Use wholemeal flour instead of white flour.
- Add breadcrumbs as a topping.

Explanation
- Increase intake of total complex carbohydrate/fruit and vegetables/bread/breakfast cereal/rice/pasta/potatoes.
- Increase intake of total complex carbohydrate foods by 25%.

(b) *2 marks*

Advantages for the consumer
- Consumers get fresh, healthy produce at competitive prices/products are usually organic and considered healthier.
- They offer increased choice, and can offer extra fresh, affordable produce in areas with few options.
- Good for the environment, as food travels less there are fewer 'food miles'/food has less packaging.
- Many consumers enjoy the atmosphere and experience at farmers markets.
- Good for the local economy and the money spent circulates in the consumers' locality.
- Reinforce local job and business networks, maintaining local employment which gives consumers more income to spend.

or any other relevant advantage.

Disadvantages for the consumer
- Seasonality — farmers sell the products and goods according to season, some products may not be available to the consumer that they require.
- Going to several different stalls/places can be time consuming and not convenient to the consumer.
- Farmers markets are usually on one day per week/fortnight and this limits when the consumer can shop/may not fit in within lifestyle/shift patterns.
- Cash is usually the only accepted payment method and may not suit consumer spending.

or any other relevant disadvantage.

(c) *2 marks*

Benefits to the consumer of cook-chill products
- The consumer has a wide range of food items to select from with this process, and so consumer choice is widened.
- Foods are usually easy to use, prepare and cook and so are suitable for many consumers who want to save time.
- Many are microwaveable and so suit the consumer who needs food quickly or who does not have many food-preparation skills.
- Foods are generally of a high quality as foods used in this process can only be used in their best condition. Therefore the consumer is usually purchasing a high-quality product.
- Some chilled products are microwaveable and, therefore, require less energy in cooking, which reduces fuel costs to the consumer.
- Some chilled products can be heated by the microwave in their original packaging which requires less equipment and can save on the washing up for consumers.
- Manufacturers have responded to the demand for 'healthier' food ranges and vegetarian options and so consumer choice is widened.
- Cook-chill foods are produced in small portion sizes and are useful for single people as they can work out cheaper than buying individual ingredients to make the same dish
- There is no loss of nutrients. Food is usually cooked first and then chilled to just above freezing — this is done very quickly and, therefore, there is less loss of nutrients for the consumer.
- Chilling does not affect food quality, colour, flavour, texture or nutritional value and, therefore, product is very acceptable to the consumer.

- Throughout production only the best quality foods are used and strict hygiene conditions prevent food poisoning.
- Chilling is not as expensive a process as freezing since less energy is required; therefore it should be slightly cheaper for the consumer.

NATIONAL 5 HEALTH AND FOOD TECHNOLOGY MODEL PAPER 3

1. (a) *2 marks*
    Reasons why a manufacturer might develop a new product:
    Any 2 reasons relating:
    - to fill a gap in the market
    - as a result of market research
    - in response to consumer complaints/suggestions
    - to counteract falling sales
    - to match a competitor's product
    - to take advantage of technological innovations
    - to take advantage of new trends
    - to increase market share.

    (b) (i) *1 mark*
        Most suitable — **Burger C**

    (ii) *3 marks*
        Varieties available (beef, chicken, quorn)
        - Has the best variety (3 available) so should suit all consumers/members of the family.
        - Has a quorn option so should suit vegetarian consumers/members of the family who are vegetarian.

        Burger weight (50g and 100g)
        - has two sizes of burger so this will be suitable for all consumers/members of the family.

        Value for money (3 stars)
        - 3 stars/best so the catering company will make a profit.
        - 3 stars/best so the catering company can price their product competitively.
        - 3 stars/best so the consumer will be more likely to buy/make repeat purchases.

        Storage details (frozen, can be cooked from frozen)
        - Frozen burgers so any that are not used will not be wasted.
        - Frozen burgers so company can buy in enough stocks without fear of waste.
        - Frozen burgers so company will be able to buy stocks in advance.
        - Can be cooked from frozen therefore (not having to allow time for defrosting) the consumer will not have to wait/queues will be avoided.

        Aesthetic appeal (4 stars)
        - 4 stars/best rating for aesthetic appeal so the consumer/family will buy/enjoy this burger.
        - 4 stars/best rating for aesthetic appeal so the consumer/family will make repeat purchases.
        - 4 stars/best rating for aesthetic appeal so company will sell more/make a greater profit.

    (c) *4 marks*
        Nutrient – Protein
        Explanation
        - growth, repair and maintenance of body tissues
        - secondary source of energy

        Nutrient – Calcium
        Explanation
        - helps build strong bones and teeth
        - helps the blood to clot
        - helps with muscle control

Nutrient – Fat
Explanation
- source of energy for the body
- warmth
- protection of internal organs
- provides fat-soluble vitamins (A,D,E and K)

Nutrient – Vitamin K
Explanation
- assists in the clotting of blood
- linked to the development of strong bones

Nutrient – Phosphorous
Explanation
- helps build strong bones and teeth
- helps to release energy from foods

Nutrient – Vitamin D
Explanation
- assists with bone and tooth development
- required for effective blood clotting
- assists in absorption of calcium

Nutrient – Vitamin B2 (milk)
Explanation
- release of energy from protein, carbohydrate and fat
- maintains healthy skin and eyes

Nutrient – Vitamin A (full cream milk)
Explanation
- assists with bone and tooth development
- promotes good night vision
- maintains healthy skin/membranes/resist infection

2. (a) **Energy — 2.02MJ**
- -ive — More than the required amount. As Susan has had to give up work she may be less likely to burn off the excess energy, increasing her chances of obesity/energy could be converted to fat.
- -ive — More than the required amount and as she spends a lot of time reading she may be less likely to burn off the excess energy, increasing her chances of obesity/energy could be converted to fat.
- -ive — More than the required amount and as she is 5 months pregnant the excess energy could be converted to fat/lead to obesity and this may cause complications at the birth/contribute to post-natal depression following the birth.
- +ive — more than the required amount but as she is 5 months pregnant the small amount of extra energy could be used for growth and development of the foetus.

Fibre — 21g
- +ive — More than the required amount which will ensure that waste products/faeces are easily removed from the body and she won't be constipated during her pregnancy.
- +ive — More than the required amount which will slow down the digestive process, giving her a feeling of fullness for longer/helps prevent snacking on fatty and sugary foods (leading to obesity).
- - ive — More than the required amount and may lead to the excess NSP binding with iron — making it unavailable and resulting in anaemia during pregnancy.
- - ive — More than the required amount and may lead to the excess NSP binding with calcium, making it unavailable and resulting in osteoporosis in later life/during pregnancy.

Protein — 28g
- -ive — Less than the required amount and as Susan is a vegan she may already lack protein in her diet which could prevent repair/maintenance of her body tissues/prevent repair during childbirth/cause poor development/growth of the baby.
- -ive — Less than the required amount and as protein can be used as a secondary source of energy Susan may be tired during pregancy/childbirth.

Iron — 9.8mg
- -ive — Less than the required amount which may result in anaemia/tiredness/lack of concentration during pregnancy.
- -ive — Less than the required amount and as Susan is a vegan/pregnant she may be deficient in iron and the lack of iron could lead to anaemia/tiredness/lack of concentration.

Calcium — 560mg
- -ive — Less than the required amount is provided and Susan has an increased need for calcium during pregnancy to help form the baby's bones so she may be more prone to osteoporosis/bones/teeth becoming brittle.
- -ive — Less than the required amount is provided and as a vegan she may be deficient in calcium (from dairy foods) and this lack of calcium could lead to osteoporosis.
- -ive — Less than the required amount is provided which could lead to excess blood loss during labour/difficult labour.
- -ive — Less than the required amount is provided and the baby will scavenge the calcium from Susan's bones leaving her with a higher risk of osteoporosis/bones/teeth becoming brittle.
- -ive — Less than the required amount is provided and the baby will scavenge the calcium from Susan's bones which may result in the baby having poor bone/teeth development.

Vitamin C — 44mg
- +ive — More than the required amount and the excess will help with the absorption of iron so Susan may be less likely to suffer from anaemia/tiredness/lack of concentration during her pregnancy
- +ive — More than the required amount and the excess Vitamin C can help reduce the risk of Susan suffering from CHD/cancer in later life.
- +ive — More than the required amount, which will ensure that through her pregnancy the baby's connective tissue/walls of blood vessels will develop/form normally.
- +ive — More than the required amount, which will help fight infections during the pregnancy.

(b) *2 marks*
Any 2 explanations relating to:
- Profiling tests/star diagrams involve the characteristics of a product being profiled and then compared with similar competitors' products. A scale of 1-5 is usually used against words to describe the product. The star diagram shape can have as many/few lines as required to test the product.
- Preference tests supply information about people's likes and dislikes for a food product. They are not intended to evaluate specific characteristics.

- Ranking tests ask the taster to rank a range of similar food products in order of preference.
- Rating tests score products on a 5- or 9-point scale according to a product's palatability appeal. Samples can be scored to evaluate specific characteristics, e.g. colour, flavour, aroma, overall acceptability and quality.
- Discrimination tests are used to evaluate the difference between similar products/evaluate specific attributes and check that a food product meets its original specification.
- Paired comparison test asks tasters to compare two samples for a specific characteristic.
- Duo-trio test asks tasters to compare three samples, one of which is the control, and how the other two are similar/different.
- Triangle tests ask tasters to identify which two samples out of three are similar.

(c) *2 marks*

Functional properties of plain flour
- Gluten stretches and forms the structure of the pastry for the quiche.
- Wholemeal flour adds nutty flavour/crunchy texture.

Functional properties of egg
- Used to produce golden brown colour in the filling.
- Sets and thickens the fillings (when protein coagulates).
- Bind the other ingredients in the quiche together.

3. (a) (i) *1 mark*
Correct choice — **Fruit ice lolly B**

(ii) *3 marks*
Sweetness 3/satisfactory
- Sweetness is 3/satisfactory so will be sweet enough for children/children will like it.
- Sweetness is 3/satisfactory/not too sweet so parents may be more likely to buy this for their children.
- Sweetness is 3/satisfactory may promote this as healthy, encouraging sales.

Shape — 5/very good/best
- 5/excellent/best rating so will make it attractive to children/encourage children to buy.
- 5/excellent/best rating so will encourage repeat sales.

Fruit flavour — 4/good/second best rating
- 4/good/second best rating so children will enjoy it/most children like fruit.
- 4/good/second best rating so will encourage repeat sales.
- 4/good/second best rating, so parents may perceive this as healthy so may be more likely to buy.

Colour — 4/good/second best rating
- 4/good/second best rating will make it attractive to children/encourage children to buy.
- 4/good/second best rating/may encourage parents to buy as it may not be too brightly coloured.

Texture — 5/excellent/best rating
- 5/excellent/best rating so children will enjoy the product.
- 5/excellent/best rating so will encourage repeat sales.
- 5/excellent/best rating will help the product maintain its unique shape.

(b) *2 marks*
Nutritional Knowledge
- +ive — Parents' food choice may be influenced by knowledge of the nutritional content of foods and the effects on health.
- +ive — Parents may have a greater knowledge of nutrition due to media promotion of healthy eating and purchase foods advised.
- -ive — Nutritional labelling on food may not be easily understood by some parents, and so may not help them to make healthy choices.

Budget
- -ive — If budget is limited more high fat and sugar foods may be chosen as they are generally cheaper to purchase.
- -ive — Fruit and vegetables may not be purchased due to fear of waste if parents are on a limited budget.
- ive — New foods may not be chosen by parents for fear of waste if money is limited.
- -ive — Single-parent families may be on a limited budget and purchase convenience foods that are high in fat/sugar.
- -ive — If two parents work more money may be available to buy more ready meals and convenience foods and these could be higher in fat and sugar.
- +ive — Ready-made meals can cost less than the total cost of ingredients if each is purchased separately.
- +ive — If two parents work in a household, then the increased income could mean that their diet could be very healthy and varied if a selection of 'healthy' foods is chosen.

(c) *3 marks*
Advantages to consumers of food additives
- Nutrients such as vitamins and minerals can be added to fortify products, making a more nutritious product for the consumer.
- The aesthetic value of the food is improved by the addition of additives such as colourings.
- An increased range of foods are available in an easy-to-prepare convenience form. This is useful for consumers who are busy and have less time to spend preparing foods than in the past.
- Foods have a longer shelf-life and so the consumer can store the products for a longer period of time /reduce waste.
- Prevents the consumer having to do a lot of shopping daily, as foods can be safely bought and stored for an extended period of time.
- Flavourings and colourings replace what has been lost in the processing or give the food qualities it did not have before.
- Uniform products are produced during large-scale manufacture.
- There is a permitted list of additives which have been tested and, therefore, the consumer can be reassured about the safety of the product.

Disadvantages of food additives to the consumer
- New additives are expensive to develop — this can mean that the higher cost is passed onto the consumer.
- Some additives are thought to cause health problems and induce cancers.
- Some additives can cause hyperactivity in children.
- Some additives can irritate sufferers of asthma and eczema.
- Some people are sensitive to certain additives and must avoid them.

Answers are also accepted if they relate to a particular food additive.

(d) *1 mark*
Name of Organisation — The Food Standards Agency

4. (a) *3 marks*
Benefits to health of eating oily fish
- Can help to prevent coronary heart disease as contain a source of essential fatty acids/are a source of Vitamin A (an antioxidant vitamin)/Low in saturated fat/high in polyunsaturated fat.
- Can help to prevent high blood pressure/heart attack as contain a source of essential fatty acids/omega 3.
- Can help to prevent strokes as contain a source of essential fatty acids/omega 3.
- Can help prevent blood clots forming as contain a source of essential fatty acids/omega 3.
- Can help to prevent rickets as contain a source of calcium/phosphorus/Vitamin D.
- Can help to prevent osteoporosis as contain a source of calcium/phosphorus/Vitamin D.
- Can help to prevent cancers as contain a source of Vitamin A, an antioxidant vitamin.
- Can help to prevent tooth decay as contain fluoride/are low in sugar.
- Can help to prevent anaemia as contain a source of iron.
- Can help to prevent night blindness as contains a source of Vitamin A.
- Can help to prevent obesity as low in sugar and therefore low in energy.

(b) *3 marks*
List of ingredients
- The consumer can take account of likes/dislikes by comparing ingredients lists.
- The consumer can take account of allergies/intolerances by comparing ingredients lists.
- The consumer can take account of the proportion/amount of an ingredient in the product when comparing ingredients lists.
- The consumer can see if the product is suitable for a vegetarian by comparing the different ingredients in the ingredient lists.

Weight/Volume
- The consumer can check if the package contains enough for their needs/how many to buy/recipe to follow to ensure they have a sufficient amount/offers best value for money.
- So the consumer can compare prices per gram/ml/litre to get the best value for money/correct amount required.
- So the consumer can calculate value for money between products of differing weights.

Country of origin
- The consumer may wish to avoid/boycott products from a certain country.
- The consumer may wish to support a particular country's produce.

(c) (i) *1 mark*
Most suitable dish for the chef to cook — **Dish C**

(ii) *3 marks*
Main ingredients — tagliatelle, tomatoes, peppers, cheese
- The dish contains no meat or fish, so will meet the criteria/be suitable for a vegetarian.
- All ingredients are suitable for a vegetarian, so this meets the specification for the dish.

Ease of preparation — 4 stars/excellent/best
- 4 stars/excellent/best, suitable as the chef has to make it on TV so he will be able to make it easily.
- 4 stars/excellent/best, suitable as the chef will be able to get a good result/make it look appealing as this is what was required.
- 4 stars/excellent/best, suitable as this meets the requirement to be easy to prepare.
- 4 stars/excellent/best, suitable as the audience may be more likely to try it themselves/will not get bored.

Cooking time — 20 minutes/shortest cooking time
- 20 minutes/shortest cooking time, suitable as the dish will be cooked in the time allocated to the show.
- 20 minutes/shortest cooking time, suitable as the chef will not have to have another dish pre-prepared.
- 20 minutes/shortest cooking time, suitable as this meets the requirement to be quick to cook.

Flavour — 3 stars/good
- 3 stars/good, so the dish will be enjoyed by the audience.
- 3 stars/good, so the audience may be more likely to try to make it themselves.

Aesthetic appeal — 4 stars/excellent/best
- 4 stars/excellent/best, suitable as the dish will be enjoyed by the audience.
- 4 stars/excellent/best, suitable as the audience/viewers may want to try to make it themselves.
- 4 stars/excellent/best, suitable as the dish will appeal to the audience/viewers.
- 4 stars/excellent/best, suitable as this is what the TV company wants.

Cost — £££/one of the least expensive
- £££/one of the least expensive, suitable as the TV company may be on a restricted budget.
- £££/one of the least expensive, suitable as the audience/viewers may be more likely to try to make it themselves.
- £££/one of the least expensive, suitable as this meets the requirement to be inexpensive.

5. (a) *6 marks*

Current Dietary Advice — **Double the intake of fruit and vegetables/increase to 400g per day/eat 5 portions a day**

Practical way of meeting
- Include a piece of fruit as a snack/lunch box item rather than a cake or biscuit.
- Portion of fruit, e.g. banana, added to breakfast cereal.
- Fresh fruit pureed into drinks.
- A variety of vegetables in soup which could be pureed.
- Extra veg on pizzas, in stews, etc.
- Add extra vegetables to main dishes, e.g. vegetable curry, bolognese.
- Served with main dishes or in salads.
- Salad used to fill sandwiches or served as an accompaniment.
- Choose fruit juices rather than fizzy drinks.
- Add to baked products for natural sweetness rather than sugar e.g raisins.

Current Dietary Advice — **Increase intake of total complex carbohydrates by 25%/to 124g (per day)**

Practical way of meeting
- Use breakfast cereals in baking, e.g. biscuits, topping for fruit crumble or yoghurts.
- Use bread in desserts, e.g. bread pudding, summer pudding.
- Make use of new continental or foreign breads to increase variety in the diet or add interest to snacks and lunches.
- Choose wholegrain, high-fibre versions of cereals which are low in sugar, salt and fat for breakfast/lunch.
- Eat breakfast cereals as a snack.
- Increase consumption of fruit and vegetables, bread, breakfast cereals, rice and pasta (especially wholegrain).
- Increase consumption of potatoes and pulse vegetables.
- Include a variety of breads, pastas, rice and cereal in the diet (especially wholegrain varieties).
- Slice bread thick when making sandwiches etc.
- Serve sandwiches as a snack or packed lunches.

Current Dietary Advice — **Double the intake of breakfast cereals/to 34g (per day)**

Practical way of meeting
- Breakfast cereals can be used in baking, e.g. biscuits, topping for fruit crumble or yoghurts.
- Choose wholegrain, high-fibre versions of cereal which are low in sugar, salt and fat for breakfast.
- Breakfast cereals can be eaten as a snack and the addition of milk will improve the nutritional value.

Current Dietary Advice — **Intake of (NME) sugar by children to reduce by half/to less than 10% of food energy/adult intake to stay the same.**

Practical way of meeting
- Check food labels before buying to check for low sugar content.
- Choose tins of fruit in natural juice rather than syrup.
- select non-sweetened versions of water/diet fizzy drinks.
- Eat fewer cakes, biscuits, sweets — hidden sugars.
- Eat wholegrain, high-fibre breakfast cereals that are low in sugar.
- Eat fresh fruit and vegetables as snacks.

- Do not give sweets as a reward to children.
- Do not add sugar to tea, coffee or cereals.
- Use sugar alternatives to sweeten foods e.g sweeteners/dried fruit etc.

Current Dietary Advice — **No more than 35% of food energy from (total) fat/no more than 11% of food energy from saturated fat**

Practical way of meeting
- Choose a healthy method of cooking, e.g. grilling, where the fat runs off, or steaming or microwaving where there is no added fat.
- Use oils and spreads sparingly and choose vegetable varieties instead of animal (e.g. olive oil instead of lard).
- Choose lean meat — cut off any extra fat. before cooking.
- Choose fish or white meat instead of red meat as it contains less saturated fat.
- Choose low-fat versions of dairy produce e.g. low-fat yoghurt, semi-skimmed/skimmed milk, low-fat butter.
- Choose cottage or edam cheese instead of cheddar.
- Check labels for fat content before buying prepared or convenience foods.
- Avoid eating too many cakes, biscuits, chocolate, crisps and savoury snacks, which all contain hidden fats.
- Avoid processed meats which are high in fat and often used in ready-made meals.

Current Dietary Advice — **Intake of bread to increase by 45% (especially wholemeal and brown)/4-6 slices (per day)**

Practical way of meeting
- Use bread when coating foods before baking/frying (wholegrain varieties preferable).
- Use bread (including stale bread) in desserts, e.g. bread pudding, summer pudding.
- Cut bread thick when preparing sandwiches as a snack or for packed lunches.
- Add breadcrumbs when making burgers/meatballs etc.
- Serve a variety of different bread with all main meals (especially wholemeal varieties).

Current Dietary Advice — **Reduce salt intake from 163mmol to 100mmol (per day)/6g (per day)**

Practical way of meeting
- choose tinned vegetables, pulses, fish that are labelled 'no added salt'.
- Limit intake of processed foods, including ham and bacon as these contain hidden salt.
- Choose low-salt alternatives e.g. lo-salt.
- Limit intake of salty snacks, e.g. crisps and peanuts — Eat fruit etc instead as a snack
- Check food labels on products for hidden salt before buying.
- Use herbs and spices for flavouring instead of salt.
- Taste food before adding salt.
- Do not have salt available on the dinner table.
- Gradually cut down the amount of salt added to food during cooking.

(b) *2 marks*

Advantages to shopping online
- Can easily 'window shop' — research/compare brands and prices without pressure from salesperson/obligation to buy.

- Can shop at any time of the day or night (suits people working shift patterns) and from the comfort of home.
- Tend to buy what you need rather than what you want which can help save money (children often contribute to this).
- Goods are delivered straight to the door which saves time travelling to and from shop.
- Delivery times can be selected which are convenient to the shopper.
- It can be cheaper as there are sometimes special internet discounts available.
- Can save time for people with busy lifestyles/ reduce travelling time/reduce travelling cost (sometimes free delivery).
- Useful for people who are housebound or disabled as they can still choose their own products.

or any other relevant advantage.

Disadvantages to shopping online
- Delivery charges can increase the cost of the goods and may be problematic if on a budget.
- Unable to actually see/touch the goods with the computer screen perhaps not showing the quality and size exactly.
- Returning goods if unsuitable can be off-putting, e.g. poor-quality vegetables, shelf-life too short.
- Some consumers like to speak to someone for advice/specialist knowledge on their purchase.
- Cash can't be used as a payment method and not everyone has a debit/credit card. Some people may be hesitant to use credit/debit cards as a form of payment, especially on unsecured websites due to fraud.
- Elderly people can often be lonely and online shopping is completed in solitary conditions.

or any other relevant disadvantage.

(c) *2 marks*
- Brush teeth at least twice a day using a fluoride toothpaste.
- Don't give children sweets when they have been upset or hurt themselves or as a reward. This will encourage a sweet tooth in later life.
- Avoid sugary foods and drinks, especially between meals. Water is the preferred drink.
- Diet drinks should be consumed as opposed to varieties containing sugar. (However, these are a major cause of tooth erosion (tooth wear) due to the acidity of the drinks).
- Foods rich in calcium, phosphorus and vitamin D should be eaten to give teeth their hardness.
- Crunchy foods, like apples and carrots, should be eaten regularly to exercise the gums and prevent infection/tooth caries.
- Eating too much salt/sodium in the diet could lead to extraction of calcium from the bone, thereby weakening the teeth/causing dental caries/decay.
- Reduce NME sugar intake by limiting consumption of sugar, sugary foods and drinks which cause a build-up of plaque which attack the enamel/ avoiding sugary and sticky snacks between meals as this causes a build-up of plaque.
- increase the use of fresh or dried fruit as sweetening agents on breakfast cereals, in baking and also as a snack food.
- Choose low-sugar varieties from vending machines/ tuckshops.